WHEN IN DOUBT, TELL THE TRUTH

Famous Lines
The Columbia Dictionary of Familiar Quotations
by Robert Andrews

The Columbia Dictionary of Quotations
by Robert Andrews

Women's Words
The Columbia Book of Quotations by Women
by Mary Biggs

Family Wisdom
The 2,000 Most Important Things Ever Said about Parenting,
  Children, and Family Life
by Susan Ginsberg

I Can Resist Everything Except Temptation
And Other Quotations from Oscar Wilde
by Karl Beckson

Of the People, By the People, For the People
And Other Quotations from Abraham Lincoln
by Gabor Borritt

Not Bloody Likely
And Other Quotations from Bernard Shaw
by Bernard Dukore

Hitch Your Wagon to a Star
And Other Quotations from Ralph Waldo Emerson
by Keith Frome

Simplify, Simplify
And Other Quotations from Henry David Thoreau
by K.P. Van Anglen

WHEN IN DOUBT, TELL THE TRUTH

And Other Quotations from MARK TWAIN

Brian Collins

Columbia University Press
New York

Columbia University Press
Publishers Since 1893
New York   Chichester, West Sussex

Library of Congress Cataloging-in-Publication Data

Twain, Mark, 1835–1910.
    When in doubt, tell the truth : and other quotations from Mark Twain /
(collected by) Brian Collins.
    p. cm.
    Includes bibliographical references.
    1. Twain, Mark, 1835–1910—Quotations. 2. Quotations, American.
I. Collins, Brian, 1960–   . II. Title.
PS1303.C65 1996   96-33235
818'. 409--dc20   CIP

Casebound editions of Columbia University Press books are printed on
permanent and durable acid-free paper.
Printed in the United States of America
c 10 9 8 7 6 5 4 3 2 1

CONTENTS

INTRODUCTION

In the volume that follows, one can see that America's favorite aphorist was preoccupied with five general concerns: human nature, history, the American scene, the art of the writer, and the tradition of the maxim itself. The reflections on human nature are dominated by the now infamous pessimism of Mark Twain's later years. Humans, he thought, are ruled by an instinctual nature irrevocably corrupted by millennia of degradation (feudalism, slavery, the Church, etc.): "The average man is what his environment and his superstitions have made him; and their function is to make him an ass." This pessimistic Twain will have no part of the Enlightenment notion that Reason can break this spell: "When the human race has once acquired a superstition nothing short of death is ever likely to remove it." Moral imperatives are equally ineffectual; indeed, where base impulses are so strong, the "Moral Sense" becomes their unwitting accomplice: "There is a Moral Sense, and there is an Immoral Sense. History shows us that the Moral Sense enables us to perceive morality and how to avoid it, and that the Immoral Sense enables us to perceive immorality and how to enjoy it." As if to illustrate the point, Twain gives us "Pap" Finn, whose rationalizations are almost admirable for their perfect nonchalance: "Take a chicken when you get a chance," warns Pap, "because if you don't want him yourself you can easy find somebody that does, and a good deed ain't ever forgot."

Twain's overall estimates of humanity did vary some, but they were almost always unflattering. At best, humans were ridiculous animals without the sense to get out of their own way: "It is human nature to yearn to be what we were never intended for." "A human being has a natural desire to have more of a good thing than he needs." "April 1. This is the day upon which we are reminded of what we are on the other three hundred and sixty-four." At its worst, Twain presents humanity as nothing less than monstrous: "Of all the animals, man is the only one that is cruel. He is the only one that inflicts pain for the pleasure of doing it." "If the desire to kill and the opportunity to kill came always together, who would escape hanging?" "The universal brotherhood of man is our most precious possession, what there is of it."

Curiously, however, the sort of person the misanthropic Twain attacked most often was the conformist—perhaps because he reasoned that a more independently minded creature would have been less vulnerable to corruptive social forces. Everywhere he saw thought and action being subordinate to mainstream views, unexamined tradition, received wisdom, and the ideals of official culture and its purveyors. "In religion and politics people's beliefs and convictions are in almost every case gotten at second-hand, and without examination, from authorities who have not themselves examined the questions at issue but have taken them at second hand from other non-examiners, whose opinions about them were not worth a brass farthing." "We all do no end of feeling, and we mistake it for thinking. And out of it we get an aggregation which we consider a boon. Its name is Public Opinion. It is held in reverence. It settles everything. Some think it is the Voice of God." "Each man is afraid of his neighbor's disapproval—a thing which, to the general run of the race, is more dreaded than wounds and death."

When one turns from Twain's reflections on human nature to his reflections on history, the conclusions are often the same—humans are still on the whole a miserable lot. But a historical perspective allows him to make comparative judgments, and the recognition that the race has made some progress gives rise to less gloomy thinking. Perhaps Reason played some role in human affairs after all? Here Twain veers away from turn-of-the-century nihilism back toward the buoyant liberalism that had flourished in the immediate aftermath of the Civil War.

Not surprisingly, the favorite targets of the liberalist Twain were the socio-political institutions of the past: "It is enough to make a body ashamed of his race to think of the sort of froth that has always occupied its thrones without a shadow of right or reason, and the seventh-rate people that have always figured as its aristocracies—a company of monarchs and nobles who, as a rule, would have achieved only poverty and obscurity if left, like their betters, to their own designs." "A privileged class, an aristocracy, is but a band of slaveholders under another name." "The Autocrat of Russia possesses more power than any other man in the earth; but he cannot stop a sneeze."

Twain was also unsparing in his scorn for what he took to be the cultural concomitant of such social arrangements, namely "superstition." From the standpoint of a resolutely rational modernity the whole length and breadth of premodern belief, especially religious belief, were supported by nothing but a series of cheap tricks, the stock in trade of hucksters like the Merlin of his novel *A Connecticut Yankee*. "A prophet doesn't have to have any brains. They are good to have, of course, for the ordinary exigencies of life, but they are of no use in professional work. It is the restfulest vocation there is. When the spirit of prophecy comes upon you, you merely cake your intellect and lay it off in a cool place for a rest, and unship your jaw and leave it alone; it will work for itself: the result is prophecy." "As for the bones of St. Denis, I feel certain we have seen enough of them to duplicate him, if necessary." Not surprisingly, one also discerns a strong antipathy for anything smacking of the chivalric code, as in his fuming about dueling: "I thoroughly disapprove of duels. I consider them unwise and I know they are dangerous. Also, sinful. If a man should challenge me now I would go to that man and take him kindly and forgivingly by the hand and lead him to a quiet retired spot and kill him."

Having noted Twain's preference for modern civilization, it should be added that he also quite demonstratively refused to have any part of what has been called the "cult of progress," from the standpoint of which the "contemporary" and the "superior" were interchangeable terms. To his mind the nineteenth century—for all of its relative merits—still left a great deal to be desired, and these qualms should not be confused with his low opinion of human nature. Modernity was very much an unfinished project for Twain; the damnable past had yet to be entirely expunged. These feelings are clearest where Twain strives to deflate civilization's exaggerated sense of its own achievement. His favorite tactic is to point out that civilization's perfection was most uncertain precisely where it was supposed to be most obvious—vis-à-vis the "savage": "He [the savage] was naked and not ashamed, now he is clothed and knows how to be ashamed; he was unenlightened, now he has a Waterbury watch; he was unrefined, now he has jewelry, and something to make him smell good." "Two or three centuries from now it will be recognized that all the competent killers are Christians; then the pagan world will go to school to the Christians: not to acquire his religion, but his guns." "There are many humorous things in the world; among them the white man's notion that he is less savage than the other savages."

This historical outlook just outlined—call it qualified progressivism—also lies behind much of what Twain has to say about America and Americans, two of Twain's favorite topics. No less than the nineteenth century, America and things American were identified with progress, and Twain himself shared this view: if the best thing that modern, western civilization had to offer was liberalism—in politics, economy, and culture—

then America was surely the apotheosis of the modern. But the idea that modernity was an unfinished project seemed to apply just as well here: "This atrocious doctrine of allegiance to party plays directly into the hands of politicians of the baser sort—and doubtless for that it was borrowed—or stolen—from the monarchical system." "Ours is the 'land of the free'— nobody denies that—nobody challenges it. (Maybe it is because we won't let other people testify.)" "We have a criminal jury system which is superior to any in the world; and its efficiency is only marred by the difficulty of finding twelve men every day who don't know anything and can't read." "The motto ['In God We Trust'] stated a lie. If this nation ever trusted in God, that time has gone by; for nearly half a century almost its entire trust has been in the Republican party and the dollar—mainly the dollar." "We've got so much taxation. I don't know of a single foreign product that enters this country untaxed except the answer to prayer." "So far as I have observed, the most striking, the most prominent, the most American of all American characteristics is the poverty of [politeness] in the American character." "When I think of some of our shipments to [hell] I realize that I should feel more or less at home there. It wouldn't surprise me there to recognize our American twang here and there." "July 4. Statistics show that we lose more fools on this day than in all other days of the year put together. This proves, by the number left in stock, that one Fourth of July per year is now inadequate, the country has grown so." "Suppose you were an idiot. And suppose you were a member of Congress. But I repeat myself."

Another rich vein of thought within this volume reflects six decades of literary experience. As one might expect Twain has a good deal to say about the craft of writing, offering advice on everything from routine stylistic matters ("As to the Adjective: when in doubt, strike it out.") to the more complicated tasks of making good literature: "There are some books that refuse to be written. They stand their ground year after year and will not be persuaded. It isn't because the book is not there and worth being written— it is only because the right form for the story does not present itself. There is only one right form for a story and if you fail to find that form the story will not tell itself." But his wisdom extends beyond technical matters to more elusive problems like that of inspiration and humor: "A book is pretty sure to get tired along about the middle and refuse to go on with its work until its powers and its interests should have been refreshed by a rest and its depleted stock of raw materials reinforced by lapse of time." "The secret source of Humor itself is not joy but sorrow. There is no humor in heaven." There are also several memorable observations concerning literature as a profession: "How often we recall, with regret, that Napoleon once shot at a magazine editor and missed him and killed a publisher. But we remember with charity that his intentions were good." And as a literary man whose work so often took him on the lecture circuit, Twain is a rich source of wisdom concerning public speaking: "Written things are not for speech; their form is literary; they are stiff, inflexible and will not lend themselves to happy and effective delivery with the tongue—where their purpose is to merely entertain, not instruct; they have to be limbered up, broken up, colloquialized and turned into the common forms of unpremeditated talk." "You ought never to have any part of the audience behind you; you can never tell what they are going to do."

The last important strand of Twain's aphoristic work consists of an assault on the maxim itself, along with the bourgeois cult of self-discipline upon which it fed. Once instrumental to the rise of a society of sovereign individuals, the cult of self-discipline had by Twain's time become one more hollow orthodoxy, emphasizing respectability rather than rectitude, and the enemy of too much that gave dimension to existence—usually, though not openly, in the interest of crude, pecuniary concerns. As a maker of "anti-maxims" Twain favored two distinct approaches. On the one hand he pointed out the altogether shallow depths of bourgeois morality: "Virtue never has been as respectable as money." "Honesty is the best policy—when there is money in it." "Prosperity is the best protector of principle." On the other hand he created maxims for a kind of counter culture: "Franklin said once, in one of his inspired flights of malignity: 'Early to bed and early to rise/Makes a man healthy and wealthy and wise.' As if it were any object to a boy to be healthy and wealthy and wise on such terms." "Diligence is a grand thing, but taking things easy is much more—restful." "I always take it [whiskey] at night as a preventive of toothache. I have never had the toothache; and what is more, I never intend to have it."

Human nature, progress, America, writing, and middle-class virtue—these interests define only the general contours of a body of work that covers a rich array of more specific topics from "advertising" to "watermelon." What ties this marvelous miscellany together, of course, is Twain's singular style, in which the insight and economy of a master-aphorist are enriched with the wit and native diction of America's greatest humorist.

ABSTINENCE ✳ ✳ ✳ ✳

Taking the pledge will not make bad liquor good, but it will improve it.

"More Maxims of Mark," *Mark Twain: Collected Tales, Sketches, Speeches, & Essays, 1891-1910*, p. 946. Library of America (1992).

ACQUITTAL

The mere failure to satisfy the exacting forms of law and prove a man guilty in a *court*, is a hundred thousand miles from proving him innocent.

"Consistency," *Mark Twain's Speeches*, p. 128. Gabriel Wells (1923). Written in 1884.

ADAM AND EVE

[Adam] was the author of sin—and I wish he had taken out an international copyright on it.

Mark Twain's Notebooks and Journals, vol. 3, p. 15. University of California (1979). Written spring 1883–September 1884.

Adam and Eve had many advantages, but the principal one was, that they escaped teething.

Pudd'nhead Wilson and Those Extraordinary Twins, ch. 4 (1894).

ADJECTIVES

As to the Adjective: when in doubt, strike it out.

"Pudd'nhead Wilson's Calendar," *Pudd'nhead Wilson*, ch. 11, p. 83. Gabriel Wells (1923). Written in 1894.

*A*DVENTURE

I've seen it in books; and so of course that's what we've got to do.

> *Adventures of Huckleberry Finn*, ch. 2, p. 12. Gabriel Wells (1923). Written in 1885.

*A*DVERSITY

By trying we can easily learn to endure adversity. Another man's, I mean.

> "Pudd'nhead Wilson's New Calendar," *Following the Equator*, ch. 39 (1897).

*A*DVERTISING

Many a small thing has been made large by the right kind of advertising.

> *A Connecticut Yankee in King Arthur's Court*, ch. 22, p. 202. Gabriel Wells (1923). Written in 1889.

*A*DVICE

A private should preserve a respectful attitude toward his superiors, and should seldom or never proceed so far as to offer suggestions to his general in the field. If the battle is not being conducted to suit him, it is better for him to resign. By the etiquette of war, it is permitted to none below the rank of newspaper correspondent to dictate to the general in the field.

> "The Benefit of Judicious Training," *Mark Twain: Collected Tales, Sketches, Speeches, & Essays, 1852-1890*, p. 774. Library of America (1992). Written in 1881.

Franklin said once in one of his inspired flights of malignity—
Early to bed and early to rise
Make a man healthy and wealth and wise.
As if it were any object to a boy to be healthy and wealthy and wise on such terms.

> "The Late Benjamin Franklin," *Mark Twain: Collected Tales, Sketches, Speeches, & Essays, 1852-1890*, p. 426. Library of America (1992). Written in 1870.

AFFECTION

Praise is well, compliment is well, but affection—that is the last and final and most precious reward that any man can win.

"Books, Authors, and Hats," *Mark Twain's Speeches*, p. 343. Gabriel Wells (1923). Speech, June 25, 1907.

AFTERLIFE, THE ⚞

When I reflect upon the number of disagreeable people who I know have gone to a better world, I am moved to lead a different life.

"Pudd'nhead Wilson's Calendar," *Pudd'nhead Wilson*, ch. 13, p. 108. Gabriel Wells (1923). Written in 1894.

I have never seen what seemed to me an atom of proof that there is a future life. And yet—I am strongly inclined to expect one.

Quoted in *Mark Twain: A Biography*, vol. 3, p. 1431. Gabriel Wells (1923).

AGE AND AGING

I have long ago lost my belief in immortality—also my interest in it.

The Autobiography of Mark Twain, ch. 49, p. 271. Harper & Row (1959).

When I was younger I could remember anything, whether it had happened or not; but my faculties are decaying now and soon I shall be so I cannot remember any but the things that never happened. It is sad to go to pieces like this but we all have to do it.

The Autobiography of Mark Twain, p. 96. Gabriel Wells (1925).

If you find that you can't make seventy by any but an uncomfortable road, don't you go. When they take off the Pullman and retire you to the rancid smoker, put off your things, count your checks, and get out at the first way station where there's a cemetery.

"Seventieth Birthday Speech," *Mark Twain: Collected Tales, Sketches, Speeches, & Essays, 1891-1910*, p. 715. Library of America (1992).

AGE AND AGING: THE FORTIES

The man who is a pessimist before 48 knows too much; if he is an optimist after it, he knows too little.

     Notebook, ch. 33, entry for December 1902, ed. Albert Bigelow Paine (1935).

ALCOHOL ⚹⚹

I always take it at night as a preventive of toothache. I have never had the toothache; and what is more, I never intend to have it.

     "Letters to Satan," *Europe and Elsewhere*, p. 218. Gabriel Wells (1923). Referring to Scotch whiskey. Written in 1897.

AMBITION

When I was a boy, there was but one permanent ambition among my comrades in our village on the west bank of the Mississippi River. That was, to be a steamboatman. We had transient ambitions of other sorts, but they were only transient. When a circus came and went, it left us all burning to become clowns; the first negro minstrel show that came to our section left us all suffering to try that kind of life; now and then we had a hope that if we lived and were good, God would permit us to be pirates. These ambitions faded out, each in its turn; but the ambition to be a steamboatman always remained.

     Life on the Mississippi, ch. 4 (1883). Originally published as "Old Times on the Mississippi," *Atlantic Monthly* (1874).

AMERICA AND AMERICANS

I believe the entire population of the United States—exclusive of the women—to be rotten, as far as the dollar is concerned.

     The Autobiography of Mark Twain, ch. 24, p. 132. Harper & Row (1959).

Thanksgiving Day, a function which originated in New England two or three centuries ago when those people recognized that they really had something to be thankful for—annually, not oftener—if they had succeeded in exterminating their neighbors, the Indians, during the previous twelve months.

The Autobiography of Mark Twain, vol. 1, p. 291. Gabriel Wells (1925).

Mine eyes have seen the orgy of the launching of the Sword;
He is searching out the hoardings where the stranger's wealth is stored;
He hath loosed his fateful lightnings, and with woe and death has scored;
His lust is marching on.

"Battle Hymn of the Republic (Brought Down to Date)," *A Pen Warmed-up in Hell*, p. 4. Harper & Row (1972). Written about 1900.

I beg you, sir, to observe our street pavements. They are our own invention. This is the only place in the world where the pavements consist exclusively of holes with asphalt around them. And they are the most economical in the world, because holes never get out of repair.

"Bishop Speech," *Mark Twain Speaking*, p. 593. University of Iowa Press (1976). Speech, October 1907.

Publicly, sir, we are intensely democratic, and much given to mocking at royalties and aristocracies, but privately we have that hankering after them and worship of them which has never been absent from any section of the human race.

"Bishop Speech," *Mark Twain Speaking*, p. 591. University of Iowa Press (1976). Speech, October 1907.

I am a Yankee of the Yankees—and practical; yes, and nearly barren of sentiment.

A Connecticut Yankee in King Arthur's Court, "A Word of Explanation," p. 5. Gabriel Wells (1923). Written in 1889.

In America, politics has a hand in everything.

"From the 'London Times' of 1904," *The Man that Corrupted Hadleyburg and Other Stories and Essays*, p. 133. Harper & Brothers (1900). Written in 1898.

$\mathcal{A}$NCESTRY

He was well born, as the saying is, and that's worth as much in a man as it is in a horse.

Adventures of Huckleberry Finn, ch. 18, p. 146. Gabriel Wells (1923). Huck, referring to Colonel Grangerford. First appeared in 1885.

$\mathcal{A}$NIMALS

Indecency, vulgarity, obscenity—these are strictly confined to man; he invented them. Among the higher animals there is no trace of them. They hide nothing; they are not ashamed. Man, with his soiled mind, covers himself. He will not even enter a drawing room with his breast and back naked, so alive are he and his mates to indecent suggestion. Man is "The Animal That Laughs." But so does the monkey, as Mr. Darwin pointed out; and so does the Australian bird that is called the laughing jackass. No— Man is the Animal that Blushes. He is the only one that does it—or has occasion to.

"The Lowest Animal," *Letters from the Earth*, Harper (1962).

The fact that man knows right from wrong proves his *intellectual* superiority to the other creatures; but the fact that he can *do* wrong proves his *moral* inferiority to any creatures that *cannot*.

Old Man, in "What Is Man?" Sect. 6 (1906), repr. in *Complete Essays*, ed. Charles Neider (1963).

It is just like man's vanity and impertinence to call an animal dumb because it is dumb to his dull perceptions.

"What Is Man?" *What Is Man? and Other Philosophical Writings*, p. 195. University of California (1973). Written in 1906.

$\mathcal{A}$PPEARANCES

Barring that natural expression of villainy which we all have, the man looked honest enough.

A Mysterious Visit, Complete Humourous Sketches and Tales, ed. Charles Neider (1961). Originally published 1870. Referring to a tax assessor.

Be careless in your dress if you must, but keep a tidy soul.

"Pudd'nhead Wilson's New Calendar," *Following the Equator*, vol. 1, ch. 23, p. 203. Gabriel Wells (1923). Written in 1897.

So I learned then, once and for all, that gold in its native state is but dull unornamental stuff, and that only lowborn metals excite the admiration of the ignorant with an ostentatious glitter. However, like the rest of the world, I still go on underrating men of gold and glorifying men of mica.

Roughing It, vol. 1, ch. 28, p. 228. Harper & Brothers (1899). Written in 1872.

Apprenticeships

Even Noah got no salary for the first six months—partly on account of the weather and partly because he was learning navigation.

"Two Halos,"*Mark Twain in Eruption*, p. 166. Harper & Brothers, 1940. Dictated in May 1906.

Architecture

The foreigner coming to these shores is more impressed at first by our sky-scrapers. They are new to him. He has not done anything of the sort since he built the tower of Babel. The foreigner is shocked by them. In the daylight they are ugly. They are—well, too chimneyfied and too snaggy—like a mouth that needs attention from a dentist; like a cemetery that is all monuments and no gravestones. But at night, seen from the river where they are columns towering against the sky, all sparkling with light, they are fairylike; they are beauty more satisfactory to the soul than anything man has dreamed of since the Arabian nights.

Mark Twain's Speeches, ed. William Dean Howells, Harpers (1910). Speech, December 6, 1900, to the St. Nicholas Society, New York.

Aristocracy

A jackass has that kind of strength, and puts it to a useful purpose, and is valuable to the world because he *is* a jackass; but a nobleman is not valuable because he is a jackass. It is a mixture that is always ineffectual, and should never have been attempted in the first place. And yet, once you start a mistake, the trouble is done and you never know what is going to come of it.

Hank Morgan, in *A Connecticut Yankee in King Arthur's Court*, ch. 15 (1889).

I will say this much for the nobility: that, tyrannical, murderous, rapacious, and morally rotten as they were, they were deeply and enthusiastically religious.

A Connecticut Yankee in King Arthur's Court, ch. 17, p. 136. Gabriel Wells (1923). Written in 1889.

We have to be despised by somebody whom we regard as above us, or we are not happy; we have to have somebody to worship and envy, or we cannot be content. In America we manifest this in all the ancient and customary ways. In public we scoff at titles and hereditary privilege, but privately we hanker after them, and when we get a chance we buy them for cash and a daughter.

Mark Twain's Own Autobiography, ch. 9, ed. Michael J. Kiskis. University of Wisconsin Press (1990). First published in the *North American Review*, vol. 184, no. 606 (January 4, 1907).

*A*RMOR

Well, a man that is packed away like that is a nut that isn't worth cracking, there is so little meat, when you get down to it, by comparison with the shell.

A Connecticut Yankee in King Arthur's Court, ch. 11, p. 90. Gabriel Wells (1923). Written in 1889.

*A*RMS RACE

By and by when each nation has 20,000 battleships and 5,000,000 soldiers we shall all be safe and the wisdom of statesmanship will stand confirmed.

"More Maxims of Mark," *Mark Twain: Collected Tales, Sketches, Speeches, & Essays, 1891–1910*, p. 941. Library of America (1992).

ARMY, THE

That's what an army is—a mob; they don't fight with courage that's born in them, but with courage that's borrowed from their mass, and from their officers.

Colonel Sherburn, in *Huckleberry Finn*, ch. 22 (1884).

ARROGANCE

Remark of Dr. Baldwin's concerning upstarts: We don't care to eat toadstools that think they are truffles.

"Pudd'nhead Wilson's Calendar," *Pudd'nhead Wilson*, ch. 5, p. 37. Gabriel Wells (1923). Written in 1894.

ART AND ARTISTS

These was all nice pictures, I reckon, but I didn't somehow seem to take to them, because if ever I was down a little, they always give me the fan-tods. Everybody was sorry she died, because she had laid out a lot more of these pictures to do, and a body could see by what she had done what they had lost. But I reckoned, that with her disposition, she was having a better time in the graveyard.

Huck, in *Adventures of Huckleberry Finn*, ch. 17 (1885).

I have got enough of the old masters! Brown says he has "shook" them, and I think I will shake them, too. You wander through a mile of picture galleries and stare stupidly at ghastly old nightmares done in lampblack and lightning, and listen to the ecstatic encomiums of the guides, and try to get up some enthusiasm, but it won't come.

Traveling with the Innocents Abroad, ch. 9, ed. David Morley McKeithan, University of Oklahoma Press (1958). First published in *Daily Alta California* (September 22, 1867).

I used to worship the mighty genius of Michael Angelo—that man who was great in poetry, painting, sculpture, architecture—great in every thing he undertook. But I do not want Michael Angelo for breakfast—for luncheon—for dinner—for tea—for supper—for between meals. I like a change, occasionally. In Genoa, he designed every thing; in Milan he or his pupils designed every thing; he designed the Lake of Como; in Padua, Verona, Venice, Bologna, who did we ever hear of, from guides, but Michael Angelo? In Florence, he painted every thing, designed every thing, nearly, and what he didn't design he used to sit on a favorite stone and look at, and they showed us the stone. In Pisa he designed everything but the old shot-tower, and they would have attributed that to him if it had not been so awfully out of the perpendicular. He designed the piers of Leghorn and the custom house regulations of Civita Vecchia. But, here—here it is frightful. He designed St. Peter's; he designed the Pope; he designed the Pantheon, the uniform of the Pope's soldiers, the Tiber, the Vatican, the Coliseum, the Capitol, the Tarpeian Rock, the Barberini Palace, St. John Lateran, the Campagna, the Appian Way, the Seven Hills, the Baths of Caracalla, the Claudian Aqueduct, the Cloaca Maxima—the eternal bore designed the Eternal City, and unless all men and books do lie, he painted every thing in it! . . . I never felt so fervently thankful, so soothed, so tranquil, so filled with a blessed peace, as I did yesterday when I learned that Michael Angelo was dead.

Innocents Abroad, ch. 27, American Publishing Company (1869).

The houses are from five to seven feet high, and all built upon one arbitrary plan—the ungraceful form of a dry-goods box. The sides are daubed with a smooth white plaster, and tastefully frescoed aloft and alow with disks of camel-dung placed there to dry. This gives the edifice the romantic appearance of having been riddled with cannon-balls, and imparts to it a very pleasing effect. When the artist has arranged his materials with an eye to just proportion—the small and the large flakes in alternate rows, and separated by carefully-considered intervals—I know of nothing more cheerful to look upon than a spirited Syrian fresco. Nothing in this world has such a charm for me as to stand and gaze for hours and hours upon the inspired works of these old masters.

Traveling with the Innocents Abroad, ch. 42, ed. David Morley McKeithan. University of Oklahoma Press (1958). First published in *Daily Alta California* (January 26, 1868).

We don't know any more about pictures than a kangaroo does about metaphysics. . . . To us, the great uncultivated, it is the last thing in the world to call a picture. Brown said it looked like an old fire-board.

Traveling with the Innocents Abroad, ch. 9, ed. David Morley McKeithan. University of Oklahoma Press (1958). Written about da Vinci's "Last Supper." First published in *Daily Alta California* (September 22, 1867).

$\mathcal{A}$SIA

India has 2,000,000 gods, and worships them all. In religion other countries are paupers; India is the only millionaire.

Following the Equator, ch. 43 (1897).

$\mathcal{A}$USTRALIA AND THE AUSTRALIANS

In the weltering hell of the Moorooroo plain
The Yatala Wangary withers and dies,
And the Worrow Wanilla, demented with pain,
To the Woolgoolga woodlands
Despairingly flies.

"A Sweltering Day in Australia," consisting of Australian place-names, ch. 36, *Following the Equator* (1897).

$\mathcal{A}$UTHORITY

To be vested with enormous authority is a fine thing; but to have the onlooking world consent to it is a finer.

A Connecticut Yankee in King Arthur's Court, ch. 8, p. 60. Gabriel Wells (1923). Written in 1889 .

$\mathcal{A}$UTHORS

There are three infallible ways of pleasing an author, and the three form a rising scale of compliment: 1, to tell him you have read one of his books; 2, to tell him you have read all of his books; 3, to ask him to let you read the manuscript of his forthcoming book. No. 1 admits you to his respect; No. 2 admits you to his admiration; No. 3 carries you clear into his heart.

"Pudd'nhead Wilson's Calendar," *Pudd'nhead Wilson*, ch. 11, p. 83. Gabriel Wells (1923). Written in 1894.

AVARICE

Honesty is the best policy—when there is money in it.

"Business," *Mark Twain's Speeches*, p. 236. Gabriel Wells (1923). Speech, March 30, 1901.

AWARDS

The cross of the Legion of Honor has been conferred on me. However, few escape that distinction.

A Tramp Abroad, ch. 8 (1880).

BABIES

 A soiled baby, with a neglected nose, cannot be conscientiously regarded as a thing of beauty.

"Answers to Correspondents," *Complete Humorous Sketches and Tales*, ed. Charles Neider (1961).
Twain was replying to a young mother.

You think a baby is a thing of beauty and a joy forever? Well, the idea is pleasing, but not original; every cow thinks the same of its own calf.

"Answers to Correspondents," *Sketches Old and New*, p. 90. Harper & Brothers, 1903. Written in June 1865.

We have not all had the good fortune to be ladies. We have not all been generals, or poets, or statesmen; but when the toast works down to the babies, we stand on common ground.

"The Babies," *Mark Twain's Speeches*, ed. Albert Bigelow Paine (1923). Speech, Nov. 1879.
Twain spoke at a banquet in which the fifteenth toast was, "The babies—as they comfort us in our sorrows, let us not forget them in our festivities."

BAD LUCK

Things ne'er do go smoothly in weddings, suicides, and courtships.

"Dinner Speech," *Mark Twain Speaking*, p. 483. University of Iowa Press (1976). Speech, February 7, 1906.

Every silver lining has a cloud behind it.

The Gilded Age, vol. 2, ch. 20, p. 225. Harper & Brothers (1901). Written in 1873.

*B*ANQUETS

A banquet is probably the most fatiguing thing in the world except ditchdigging.

"Last Visit to England," *Mark Twain in Eruption*, p. 320. Harper & Brothers (1940). Dictated by Twain during the summer of 1907.

*B*ARGAINING

A man pretty much always refuses another man's first offer, no matter what it is.

The Gilded Age, vol. 1, ch. 6, p. 72. Harper & Brothers (1901). Written in 1873.

*B*EAUTY

One frequently only finds out how really beautiful a really beautiful woman is after considerable acquaintance with her.

The Innocents Abroad, vol. 2, ch. 27, p. 322. Gabriel Wells (1923). Written in 1869.

We can't always have the beautiful aspect of things. Let us make the most of our sights that are beautiful and let the others go.

Mark Twain's Speeches, ed. William Dean Howells, Harpers (1910). Speech, December 6, 1900, to the St. Nicholas Society, New York.

*B*EGGARS ✳

We are all beggars, each in his own way.

Mark Twain: A Biography (Paine), vol. 3, p. 1584. Gabriel Wells (1923).

Belief

Against a diseased imagination, demonstration goes for nothing.

"The Private History of a Campaign That Failed," *A Pen Warmed-up in Hell*, p. 23. Harper & Row (1972). Written in December 1885.

Bereavement

A man's house burns down. The smoking wreckage represents only a ruined home that was dear through years of use and pleasant associations. By and by, as the days and weeks go on, first he misses this, then that, then the other thing. And when he casts about for it he finds that it was in that house. Always it is an *essential*—there was but one of its kind. It cannot be replaced. It was in that house. It is irrevocably lost. . . . It will be years before the tale of lost essentials is complete, and not till then can he truly know the magnitude of his disaster.

Autobiography, ch. 66, ed. Charles Neider (1959).

Twain was writing of the death of his daughter Susie Clemens of meningitis, Aug. 18, 1896, explaining how "a man, all unprepared, can receive a thunder-stroke like that and live. . . . It will take mind and memory months and possibly years to gather together the details and thus learn and know the whole extent of the loss."

Bible, The

It is full of interest. It has noble poetry in it; and some clever fables; and some blood-drenched history; and some good morals; and a wealth of obscenity, and upwards of a thousand lies.

Letter 3, *Letters from the Earth*, p. 14. Harper & Row (1962). Written in 1909.

Protestant parents still keep a Bible handy in the house, so that the children can study it, and one of the first things the little boys and girls learn is to be righteous and holy and not piss against the wall. They study those passages more than they study any others, except those which incite to masturbation. Those they hunt out and study in private.

Satan, in *Letters from the Earth*, p. 50, ed. Bernard DeVoto. Harpers (1942).

BICYCLES

Get a bicycle. You will not regret it. If you live.

"Taming the Bicyle," *Collected Tales, Sketches, & Essays: 1852–1890*, p. 899. Library of America (1992). Written about 1886.

BIOGRAPHY

An autobiography that leaves out the little things and enumerates only the big ones is no proper picture of the man's life at all; his life consists of his feelings and his interests, with here and there an incident apparently big or little to hang the feelings on.

The Autobiography of Mark Twain, vol. 1, p. 288. Gabriel Wells (1925).

Biographies are but the clothes and buttons of the man—the biography of the man himself cannot be written.

The Autobiography of Mark Twain, vol. 1, p. 2. Gabriel Wells (1925).

Life does not consist mainly—or even largely—of facts and happenings. It consists mainly of the storm of thoughts that is forever blowing through one's head.

The Autobiography of Mark Twain, vol. 1, p. 283. Gabriel Wells (1925).

There was never yet an uninteresting life. Such a thing is an impossibility. Inside of the dullest exterior there is a drama, a comedy, and a tragedy.

The bos'n, in *The Refuge of the Derelicts*, ch. 4 (1905–1906), repr. in *Fables of Man*, ed. John S. Tuckey (1972).

BLASPHEMY

Blasphemy? No, it is not blasphemy. If God is as vast as that, he is above blasphemy; if He is as little as that, He is beneath it.

Quoted in *Mark Twain: A Biography* (Paine), vol. 3, p. 1354. Gabriel Wells (1923).

Boasting

He was a shy as a newspaper is when referring to its own merits.

"Pudd'nhead Wilson's New Calendar," *Following the Equator*, vol. 1, ch. 6, p. 63. Gabriel Wells (1923). Written in 1897.

Boldness

The timid man yearns for full value and demands a tenth. The bold man strikes for double value and compromises on par.

"Pudd'nhead Wilson's New Calendar," *Following the Equator*, vol. 1, ch. 13, p. 118. Gabriel Wells (1923). Written in 1897.

Books

There was books too. . . . One was "Pilgrim's Progress," about a man that left his family it didn't say why. I read considerable in it now and then. The statements was interesting, but tough.

Huck, in *Adventures of Huckleberry Finn*, ch. 17 (1885).

A big leather-bound volume makes an ideal razorstrap. A thin book is useful to stick under a table with a broken caster to steady it. A large, flat atlas can be used to cover a window with a broken pane. And a thick, old-fashioned heavy book with a clasp is the finest thing in the world to throw at a noisy cat.

Quoted in *Greatly Exaggerated*, "Gifts," ed. Alex Ayres (1988).

This was Twain's reply to a lady who asked Twain if he thought a book was the most useful gift one could give.

Books: *classics*

"Classic." A book which people praise and don't read.

Following the Equator, ch. 25 (1897).

A classic—something that everybody wants to have read and nobody wants to read.

Mark Twain's Speeches, ed. Albert Bigelow Paine (1923). Speech, Nov. 20, 1900, Nineteenth Century Club, New York City.

Here quoting Professor Caleb Winchester.

Boys

The Model Boy of my time—we never had but one—was perfect: perfect in manners, perfect in dress, perfect in conduct, perfect in filial piety, perfect in exterior godliness; but at bottom he was a prig; and as far as the contents of his skull, they could have changed place with the contents of a pie, and nobody would have been worse off for it but the pie.

Life on the Mississippi, ch. 54 (1883). Originally published as "Old Times on the Mississippi," *Atlantic Monthly* (1874).

There comes a time in every rightly constructed boy's life when he has a raging desire to go somewhere and dig for hidden treasure.

Tom Sawyer, ch. 26 (1876).

Breakfast

Average American's simplest and commonest form of breakfast consists of coffee and beefsteak.

A Tramp Abroad, ch. 49 (1879).

Brotherhood

The universal brotherhood of man is our most precious possession, what there is of it.

"Pudd'nhead Wilson's New Calendar," *Following the Equator*, vol. 1, ch. 27, p. 238. Gabriel Wells (1923). Written in 1897.

*B*ROTHERS

If at any time you find it necessary to correct your brother, do not correct him with mud—never on any account throw mud at him, because it will soil his clothes. It is better to scald him a little; for then you attain two desirable results—you secure his immediate attention to the lesson you are inculcating, and, at the same time, your hot water will have a tendency to remove impurities from his person—and possibly the skin also, in spots.

"Advice for Good Little Girls,"*Early Tales and Sketches*, vol. 2, p. 244. University of California (1981). Written in 1865.

*B*UREAUCRACY

If a man lives long enough he can trace a thing through the Circumlocution Office of Washington and find out, after much trouble and delay, that which he could have found out on the first day if the business of the Circumlocution Office were as ingeniously systematized as it would be if it were a great private mercantile institution.

"The Great Beef Contract," *Sketches Old and New*, p. 131. Harper & Brothers (1903). Written in May 1870.

*B*USINESS

Knighterrantry is a most chuckleheaded trade, and it is tedious hard work, too, but I begin to see that there *is* money in it, after all, if you have luck. Not that I would ever engage in it, as a business, for I wouldn't. No sound and legitimate business can be established on a basis of speculation. A successful whirl in the knighterrantry line—now what is it when you blow away the nonsense and come down to the cold facts? It's just a corner in pork, that's all.

Hank Morgan, in *A Connecticut Yankee in King Arthur's Court*, ch. 19 (1889).

There are two times in a man's life when he should not speculate: when he can't afford it, and when he can.

Following the Equator, ch. 56 (1897).

October. This is one of the peculiarly dangerous months to speculate in stocks in. The others are July, January, September, April, November, May, March, June, December, August, and February.

"Pudd'nhead Wilson's Calendar," *Pudd'nhead Wilson*, ch. 13 (1894).

Let your secret sympathies and your compassion be always with the under dog in the fight—this is magnanimity; but bet on the other one—this is business.

Quoted in *Mark Twain: A Biography* (Paine), vol. 2, p. 705. Gabriel Wells (1923).

CAMPING

Nothing helps scenery like ham and eggs.

Roughing It, vol. 1, ch. 17, p. 148. Harper & Brothers (1899). Written in 1872.

CATS

Of all God's creatures there is only one that cannot be made the slave of the lash. That one is the cat. If man could be crossed with a cat it would improve man, but it would deteriorate the cat.

Notebook, pp. 236–237, entry for 1984, ed. Albert Bigelow Paine (1935).

A home without a cat—and a well-fed, well-petted and properly revered cat—may be a perfect home, perhaps, but how can it prove title?

Pudd'nhead Wilson, ch. 1, p. 2. Gabriel Wells (1923). Written in 1894.

CAUTION

Put all your eggs in the one basket and—WATCH THAT BASKET.

"Pudd'nhead Wilson's Calendar," *Pudd'nhead Wilson*, ch. 15 (1894).

CHARACTER

The average man is what his environment and his superstitions have made him; and their function is to make him an ass.

"At the Appetite Cure," *The Man that Corrupted Hadleyburg and Other Stories and Essays*, p. 160. Harper & Brothers (1900). Written in 1899.

It is my conviction that a person's temperament is a law, an iron law, and has to be obeyed, no matter who disapproves; manifestly, as it seems to me, temperament is a law of God.

The Autobiography of Mark Twain, ch. 63, p. 334. Harper & Row (1959).

Whenever we have a strong and persistent and ineradicable instinct we may be sure it is not original with us but inherited—inherited from away back and hardened and perfected by the petrifying influence of time.

The Autobiography of Mark Twain, ch. 5, p. 17. Harper & Row (1959).

Earn a character first if you can, and if you can't, then assume one.

"Dinner Speech," *Mark Twain Speaking*, p. 600. University of Iowa Press (1976). Speech, December 22, 1907.

To arrive at a just estimate of a renowned man's character one must judge it by the standards of his time, not ours.

Joan of Arc, preface (1896).

CHARITY

Take it all around, I was feeling ruther comfortable, on accounts of taking all this trouble for that gang, for not many would a done it. I wished the widow knowed about it. I judged she would be proud of me for helping these rapscallions, because rapscallions and dead beats is the kind the widow and good people takes the most interest in.

Huck, in *Adventures of Huckleberry Finn*, ch. 3 (1885).

By nature we are not free givers, and have to be patiently and persistently hunted down in the interest of the unfortunate.

"Concerning the Jews," *The Man that Corrupted Hadleyburg and Other Stories and Essays*, p. 257. Harper & Brothers (1900). Written in October 1899.

In all the ages, three-fourths of the support of the great charities has been conscience money.

"A Humane Word from Satan," *Collected Tales, Sketches, & Essays: 1891-1910*, p. 656. Library of America, 1992. Written on April 8, 1905.

When a person with his millions gives a hundred thousand dollars it makes a great noise in the world, but he does not miss it; it's the widow's mite that makes no noise but does the best work.

"Votes for Women," *Mark Twain's Speeches*, p. 232. Gabriel Wells (1923). Speech, February 27, 1901.

CHEERFULNESS

If there is one thing that is really cheerful in the world, it is cheerfulness. I have noticed it often. And I have noticed that when a man is right down cheerful, he is seldom unhappy for the time being. Such is the nature of man.

Traveling with the Innocents Abroad, ch. 25, ed. David Morley McKeithan. University of Oklahoma Press (1958). Originally published in *Daily Alta California* (November 3, 1867).

CHICAGO

Satan (impatiently) to Newcomer: The trouble with you Chicago people is, that you think you are the best people down here; whereas you are merely the most numerous.

"Pudd'nhead Wilson's New Calendar," *Following the Equator* ch. 60 (1897).

CHILDREN ✳

Children have but little charity for one another's defects.

The Autobiography of Mark Twain (Neider), ch. 4, p. 13. Harper & Row (1959).

Familiarity breeds contempt—and children.

Notebooks (1935).

CHRISTIANITY

Two or three centuries from now it will be recognized that all the competent killers are Christians; then the pagan world will go to school to the Christians: not to acquire his religion, but his guns.

"The Chronicle of Young Satan," *Mark Twain's Mysterious Stranger Manuscripts*, ch. 8, p. 137. University of California (1969). Written 1897–1900.

If Christ were here now, there is one thing he would *not* be—a Christian.

Mark Twain's Notebook, p. 328 . Harper & Brothers (1935). Written about 1897.

CHOICES

The election makes me think of a story of a man who was dying. He had only two minutes to live, so he sent for a clergyman and asked him, "Where is the best place to go to?" He was undecided about it. So the minister told him that each place had its advantages—heaven for climate, and hell for society.

"Tammany and Croker," *Mark Twain's Speeches*, p. 92. Harper & Brothers (1910).

CHURCH, THE

There warn't anybody at the church, except maybe a hog or two, for there warn't any lock on the door, and hogs likes a puncheon floor in summertime because it's cool. If you notice, most folks don't go to church only when they've got to; but a hog is different.

Huck, in *The Adventures of Huckleberry Finn*, ch. 18 (1885).

The church is always trying to get other people to reform; it might not be a bad idea to reform itself a little, by way of example.

A Tramp Abroad, vol. 2, ch. 7, p. 92. Harper & Brothers (1899). Written in 1880.

CITIZENSHIP

There are no private citizens in a republic. Every man is an official: above all, he is a policeman. He does not need to wear a helmet and brass buttons, but his duty is to look after the enforcement of the laws.

"Training That Pays," *Mark Twain Speaking*, p. 390. University of Iowa Press (1976). Speech, March 16, 1901.

CIVIL WAR, AMERICAN ✷✦✦✦ ! !

In the South, the war is what A.D. is elsewhere: they date from it.

Life on the Mississippi, ch. 45 (1883). Originally published as "Old Times on the Mississippi," *Atlantic Monthly* (1874).

CIVILIZATION

The widow Douglas, she took me for her son, and allowed she would sivilize me; but it was rough living in the house all the time, considering how dismal regular and decent the widow was in all her ways; and so when I couldn't stand it no longer, I lit out. I got into my old rags, and my sugar-hogshead again, and was free and satisfied. But Tom Sawyer, he hunted me up and said he was going to start a band of robbers, and I might join if I would go back to the widow and be respectable. So I went back.

Huck, in *Adventures of Huckleberry Finn*, ch. 1 (1885).

He was naked and not ashamed, now he is clothed and knows how to be ashamed; he was unenlightened, now he has a Waterbury watch; he was unrefined, now he has jewelry, and something to make him smell good.

Following the Equator, vol. 1, ch. 6, p. 65. Gabriel Wells (1923). Referring to the benefits of civilization. First appeared in 1897.

There are many humorous things in the world; among them the white man's notion that he is less savage than the other savages.

Following the Equator, vol. 1, ch. 21, p. 192. Gabriel Wells (1923).

How solemn and beautiful is the thought that the earliest pioneer of civilization, the van-leader of civilization, is never the steamboat, never the railroad, never the newspaper, never Sabbath-school, never the missionary—but always whiskey.

Life on the Mississippi, ch. 60, p. 428. Harper & Brothers (1903). Written in 1883.

Civilization is a limitless multiplication of unnecessary necessaries.

"More Maxims of Mark," *Mark Twain: Collected Tales, Sketches, Speeches, & Essays, 1891-1910*, p. 942. Library of America (1992).

CLERGY

The average clergyman could not fire into his congregation with a shotgun and hit a worse reader than himself.

A Tramp Abroad, vol. 2, ch. 7, p. 93. Harper & Brothers (1899). Written in 1880.

CLASS

She was not quite what you would call refined. She was not what you would call unrefined. She was the kind of person that keeps a parrot.

Following the Equator, ch. 57 (1897).

CLOTHES

Clothes make the man. Naked people have little or no influence in society.

"More Maxims of Mark," *Mark Twain: Collected Tales, Sketches, Speeches, & Essays, 1891-1910*, p. 942. Library of America (1992).

I never knowed how clothes could change a body before. Why, before, he looked like the orneriest old rip that ever was; but now, when he'd take off his new white beaver and make a bow and do a smile, he looked that grand and good and pious that you'd say he had walked right out of the ark, and maybe was old Leviticus himself.

Huck, in *The Adventures of Huckleberry Finn*, ch. 24 (1885).

We must put up with our clothes as they are—they have their reason for existing. They are on us to expose us—to advertise what we wear them to conceal.

Following the Equator, vol. 2, ch. 1, pp. 10–11. Gabriel Wells (1923). Written in 1897.

Their costumes, as to architecture, were the latest fashion intensified; they were rainbow-hued; they were hung with jewels—chiefly diamonds. It would have been plain to any eye that it had cost something to upholster these women.

The Gilded Age, vol. 2, ch. 2, p. 21. Harper & Brothers (1901). Referring to the dress of partygoers in Washington, D.C. First appeared in 1873.

Coconut trees

I once heard a grouty Northern invalid say that a coconut tree might be poetical, possibly it was; but it looked like a feather-duster struck by lightning.

Roughing It, vol. 2, ch. 23, p. 215. Harper & Brothers (1899). Written in 1872.

Coffee

After a few months' acquaintance with European "coffee," one's mind weakens, and his faith with it, and he begins to wonder if the rich beverage of home, with its clotted layer of yellow cream on top of it, is not a mere dream after all, and a thing which never existed.

A Tramp Abroad, ch. 49 (1880).

Colonialism

It is easier to stay out than get out.

Following the Equator, ch. 18 (1897).

[handwritten annotation: like staying in a shelter?]

Columbus

He didn't need to do anything at all but sit in the cabin of his ship and hold his grip and sail straight on, and America would discover itself. Here it was barring his passage the whole length and breadth of the South American continent, and he couldn't get by it. He'd got to discover it.

"Henry M. Stanley," *Mark Twain's Speeches*, p. 132. Gabriel Wells (1923). Referring to Columbus, November 1886.

Commonplace, the

If to be interesting is to be uncommonplace, it is becoming a question, with me, if there *are* any commonplace people.

"The Refuge of the Derelicts," *Fables of Man*, ch. 4, ed. John S. Tuckey (1972). Written 1905–1906.

Company

It is your human environment that makes climate.

"Pudd'nhead Wilson's New Calendar," *Following the Equator*, vol. 1, ch. 9, p. 89. Gabriel Wells (1923). Written in 1897.

Complaints

It is easy to find fault, if one has that disposition. There was once a man who, not being able to find any other fault with his coal, complained that there were too many prehistoric toads in it.

"Pudd'nhead Wilson's Calendar," *Pudd'nhead Wilson*, ch. 9, p. 69. Gabriel Wells (1923). Written in 1894.

Compliments

There is nothing you can say in answer to a compliment. I have been complimented myself a great many times, and they always embarrass me— I always feel that they have not said enough.

"Fulton Day, Jamestown," published in *Mark Twain's Speeches*, ed. Albert Bigelow Paine (1923). Speech, Sept. 23, 1907.

COMPOSURE

Try to keep your feelings where you can reach them with a dictionary.

"Political Economy," *Sketches Old and New*, p. 20. Harper & Brothers (1903). Written in September 1870.

CONFORMITY

This nightmare occupied some ten pages of manuscript and wound off with a sermon so destructive of all hope to non-Presbyterians that it took the first prize. This composition was considered to be the very finest effort of the evening. . . . It may be remarked, in passing, that the number of compositions in which the word "beauteous" was over-fondled, and human experience referred to as "life's page," was up to the usual average.

The Adventures of Tom Sawyer, ch. 21 (1876).

There are certain sweet-smelling sugar-coated lies current in the world which all politic men have apparently tacitly conspired together to support and perpetuate. One of these is, that there is such a thing in the world as independence.

The Autobiography of Mark Twain, vol. 2, p. 8. Gabriel Wells (1925).

Loyalty to petrified opinions never yet broke a chain or freed a human soul in *this* world—and never *will*.

"Consistency," *Mark Twain: Collected Tales, Sketches, Speeches, & Essays, 1852-1890*, p. 916. Library of America (1992). Written in 1887.

We all do no end of feeling, and we mistake it for thinking. And out of it we get an aggregation which we consider a Boon. Its name is Public Opinion. It is held in reverence. It settles everything. Some think it the Voice of God.

"Corn-Pone Opinions," *Mark Twain: Collected Tales, Sketches, Speeches, & Essays, 1891-1910*, p. 511. Library of America (1992).

You tell me whar a man gits his corn-pone, en I'll tell you what his 'pinions is.

"Corn-Pone Opinions," *Mark Twain: Collected Tales, Sketches, Speeches, & Essays, 1891-1910*, p. 507. Library of America (1992).

To create man was a quaint and original idea, but to add the sheep was tautology.

"More Maxims of Mark,, *Mark Twain: Collected Tales, Sketches, Speeches, & Essays, 1891-1910*, p. 946. Library of America (1992).

Each man is afraid of his neighbor's disapproval—a thing which, to the general run of the race, is more dreaded than wounds and death.

"The United States of Lyncherdom," *A Pen Warmed-up in Hell*, p. 156. Harper & Row (1972). Written in 1901.

CONGENIALITY

He liked to like people, therefore people liked him.

Joan of Arc, bk. 2, ch. 16, p. 174. Harper & Brothers, 1881. Written in 1896.

CONGRESS (U.S.)

It could probably be shown by facts and figures that there is no distinctly native American criminal class except Congress.

Following the Equator, ch. 8, "Pudd'nhead Wilson's New Calendar," (1897).

Suppose you were an idiot. And suppose you were a member of Congress. But I repeat myself.

Quoted in *Mark Twain: A Biography* (Paine), vol. 2, p. 274. Gabriel Wells (1923).

CONQUEST

A courteous modern phrase which means robbing your neighbor—for your neighbor's benefit.

Following the Equator, vol. 1, ch. 3, p. 29. Gabriel Wells (1923). Referring to the Hawaiian king's "enlarging his sphere of influence." First appeared in 1897.

Conscience

But that's always the way; it don't make no difference whether you do right or wrong, a person's conscience ain't got no sense, and just goes for him *anyway*. . . . It takes up more room than all the rest of a person's insides, and yet ain't no good, nohow. Tom Sawyer thinks the same.

Huck, in *Adventures of Huckleberry Finn*, ch. 33 (1885).

I thought a minute, and says to myself, hold on,—s'pose you'd a done right and give Jim up; would you felt better than what you do now? No, says I, I'd feel bad—I'd feel just the same way I do now. Well, then, says I, what's the use you learning to do right, when it's troublesome to do right and ain't no trouble to do wrong, and the wages is just the same?

Huck, in *Adventures of Huckleberry Finn*, ch. 16 (1885).

It don't make no difference whether you do right or wrong, a person's conscience ain't got no sense, and just goes for him *anyway*. If I had a yaller dog that didn't know no more than a person's conscience does, I would pison him.

Huck, in *Adventures of Huckleberry Finn*, ch. 33 (1885).

There is no real difference between a conscience and an anvil—I mean for comfort. I have noticed it a thousand times. And you could dissolve an anvil with acids, when you couldn't stand it any longer; but there isn't any way you can work off a conscience—at least so it will stay worked off.

A Connecticut Yankee in King Arthur's Court, ch. 18, p. 153. Gabriel Wells (1923). Written in 1889 .

The Moral Sense teaches us what is right, and how to avoid it—when unpopular.

"The United States of Lyncherdom," *Europe and Elsewhere*, p. 244. Gabriel Wells (1923). Written in 1901.

Consistency

What, then, is the true Gospel of consistency? Change. Who is the really consistent man? The man who changes. Since change is the law of his being, he cannot be consistent if he stick in a rut.

"Consistency," (1923). Paper, read in Hartford, Connecticut, 1884; repr. in *Complete Essays*, ed. Charles Neider (1963).

CONSTELLATIONS

Constellations have always been troublesome things to name. If you give one of them a fanciful name, it will always persist in not resembling the thing it has been named for.

Following the Equator, vol. 1, ch. 5, p. 59. Gabriel Wells (1923). Written in 1897.

CONVENTIONALITY

All human rules are more or less idiotic.

Following the Equator, ch. 50 (1897).

CONVERSATION

War talk by men who have been in a war is always interesting; whereas moon talk by a poet who has not been in the moon is likely to be dull.

Life on the Mississippi, ch. 44 (1883). Originally published as "Old Times on the Mississippi," *Atlantic Monthly* (1874).

COOPER, JAMES FENIMORE

It seems to me that *Deerslayer* is just simply a literary *delirium tremens*.

"Fenimore Cooper's Literary Offenses," *The Portable Mark Twain*, p. 556. Viking (1946). Written in 1895.

CORRUPTION

The government of my country snubs honest simplicity, but fondles artistic villainy, and I think I might have developed into a very capable pickpocket if I had remained in the public service a year or two.

Roughing It, vol. 1, ch. 25, p. 208. Harper & Brothers (1899). Written in 1872.

COURAGE

In the matter of courage we all have our limits. There never was a hero who did not have his bounds.

"Courage," *Mark Twain's Speeches*, p. 386. Gabriel Wells (1923). Speech, April 18, 1908.

To believe yourself brave is to *be* brave; it is the one only essential thing.

Joan of Arc, bk. 2, ch. 11, p. 140. Harper & Brothers, 1896. Written in 1896.

Courage is resistance to fear, mastery of fear—not absence of fear. Except a creature be part coward it is not a compliment to say it is brave; it is merely a loose application of the word. Consider the flea!—incomparably the bravest of all the creatures of God, if ignorance of fear were courage.

"Pudd'nhead Wilson's Calendar," *Pudd'nhead Wilson*, ch. 12 (1894).

COURTESY

So far as I have observed, the most striking, the most prominent, the most American of all American characteristics is the poverty of it in the American character.

"Introducing Doctor Van Dyke," *Mark Twain's Speeches*, p. 300. Gabriel Wells (1923). Referring to politeness, 1906.

COURTSHIP

The next moment he was "showing off" with all his might—cuffing boys, pulling hair, making faces—in a word, using every art that seemed likely to fascinate a girl and win her applause.

The Adventures of Tom Sawyer, ch. 4 (1876).

COWARDICE

If the bubble reputation can be obtained only at the cannon's mouth, I am willing to go there for it, provided the cannon is empty.

"A Presidential Candidate," *Mark Twain: Collected Tales, Sketches, Speeches, & Essays, 1852-1890,* p. 725. Library of America (1992). Written in 1879.

There are several good protections against temptations, but the surest is cowardice.

Following the Equator, ch. 36 (1897).

CREATION

It's lovely to live on a raft. We had the sky, up there, all speckled with stars, and we used to lay on our backs and look up at them, and discuss about whether they was made, or only just happened—Jim he allowed they was made, but I allowed they happened; I judged it would have took too long to *make* so many.

Huck, in *Adventures of Huckleberry Finn,* ch. 19 (1885).

Why *was* the human race created? Or at least why wasn't something creditable created in place of it? God had His opportunity. He could have made a reputation. But no, He must commit this grotesque folly—a lark which must have cost Him a regret or two when He came to think it over and observe effects.

Letter, Jan. 25, 1900, to W. D. Howells, repr. in *The Twain-Howells Letters,* vol. 2, eds. Henry Nash Smith and William M. Gibson (1960).

Where was the use, originally, in rushing this whole globe through in six days? It is likely that if more time had been taken, in the first place, the world would have been made right, and this ceaseless improving and repairing would not be necessary now.

Life on the Mississippi, ch. 51 (1883). Originally published as "Old Times on the Mississippi," *Atlantic Monthly* (1874).

Nothing is made in vain, but the fly came near it.

"More Maxims of Mark," *Mark Twain: Collected Tales, Sketches, Speeches, & Essays, 1891-1910,* p. 945. Library of America (1992).

CREDIT

Beautiful credit! The foundation of modern society. Who shall say that this is not the golden age of mutual trust, of unlimited reliance upon human promises? That is a peculiar condition of society which enables a whole nation to instantly recognize point and meaning in the familiar newspaper anecdote, which puts into the mouth of a distinguished speculator in lands and mines this remark:—"I wasn't worth a cent two years ago, and now I owe two millions of dollars."

The Gilded Age, ch. 26 (1873).

CRIME

A crime persevered in a thousand centuries ceases to be a crime, and becomes a virtue. This is the law of custom, and custom supersedes all other forms of law.

"Pudd'nhead Wilson's New Calendar," *Following the Equator,* ch. 63 (1897).

CRITICISM

I like criticism, but it must be my way.

The Autobiography of Mark Twain, vol. 2, p. 247. Gabriel Wells (1925).

The trade of critic, in literature, music, and the drama, is the most degraded of all.

The Autobiography of Mark Twain, vol. 2, p. 69. Gabriel Wells (1925).

One musn't criticize other people on grounds where he can't stand perpendicular himself.

A Connecticut Yankee in King Arthur's Court, ch. 26, p. 260. Gabriel Wells (1923). Written in 1889 .

The critic's symbol should be the tumble-bug: he deposits his egg in somebody else's dung, otherwise he could not hatch it.

Mark Twain's Notebook, p. 392. Harper & Brothers (1935). Written about 1904.

It is the will of God that we must have critics, and missionaries, and Congressmen, and humorists, and we must bear the burden. Meantime, I seem to have been drifting into criticism myself. But that is nothing. At the worst, criticism is nothing more than a crime, and I am not unused to that.

Mark Twain's Own Autobiography, ch. 4, ed. Michael J. Kiskis, University of Wisconsin Press (1990). First published in the *North American Review*, vol. 183, no. 601 (October 19, 1906).

CULTURE

I have witnessed and greatly enjoyed the first act of everything Wagner created, but the effect on me has always been so powerful that one act was quite sufficient; whenever I have witnessed two acts I have gone away physically exhausted; and whenever I have ventured an entire opera the result has been the next thing to suicide.

The Autobiography of Mark Twain, ch. 12, pp. 64–5. Harper & Row (1959).

CURSES

The spirit of wrath—not the words—is the sin; and the spirit of wrath is cursing. We begin to swear before we can talk.

"Pudd'nhead Wilson's New Calendar," *Following the Equator*, vol. 1, ch. 31, p. 274. Gabriel Wells (1923). Written in 1897.

CUSTOMS

Often, the less there is to justify a traditional custom, the harder it is to get rid of it.

The Adventures of Tom Sawyer, ch. 5 (1876).

DEATH AND THE DEAD

Annihilation has no terrors for me, because I have already tried it before I was born—a hundred million years—and I have suffered more in an hour, in this life, than I remember to have suffered in the whole hundred million years put together. There was a peace, a serenity, an absence of all sense of responsibility, an absence of worry, an absence of care, grief, perplexity; and the presence of a deep content and unbroken satisfaction in that hundred million years of holiday which I look back upon with a tender longing and with a grateful desire to resume, when the opportunity comes.

> *The Autobiography of Mark Twain*, ch. 50, p. 272. Harper & Row (1959).

It is one of the mysteries of our nature that a man, all unprepared, can receive a thunder-stroke like that and live.

> *The Autobiography of Mark Twain*, vol. 2, p. 34. Gabriel Wells (1925). Referring to the news that his daughter had died.

It takes *training* to enable a person to be properly courteous when he is dying. Many have tried it. I suppose very few have succeeded.

> *The Autobiography of Mark Twain*, vol. 1, p. 345. Gabriel Wells (1925).

We never become really and genuinely our entire and honest selves until we are dead—and not then until we have been dead years and years. People ought to start dead and then they would be honest so much earlier.

> *Autobiography*, ch. 55, ed. Charles Neider (1959).

All say, "How hard it is that we have to die"—a strange complaint to come form the mouths of people who have had to live.

> "Pudd'nhead Wilson's Calendar," *Pudd'nhead Wilson*, ch. 10, p. 76. Gabriel Wells (1923). Written in 1894.

Whoever has lived long enough to find out what life is, knows how deep a debt of gratitude we owe to Adam, the first great benefactor of our race. He brought death into the world.

> "Pudd'nhead Wilson's Calendar," *Pudd'nhead Wilson*, ch. 3 (1894).
>
> Twain offered further thanks to Adam in *Following the Equator*, ch. 33 (1897): "Let us be grateful to Adam, our benefactor. He cut us out of the 'blessing' of idleness and won for us the 'curse' of labor."

Debt

These annual bills! These annual bills!, How many a song their discord
trills, Of "truck" consumed, enjoyed, forgot, Since I was skinned by last
year's lot!

"Those Annual Bills," *Sketches Old and New*, p. 68. Harper & Brothers (1903). Written in 1875.

Deceit

Some authorities hold that the young ought not to lie at all. That, of
course, is putting it rather stronger than necessary; still, while I cannot go
quite so far as that, I do maintain, and I believe I am right, that the young
ought to be temperate in the use of this great art until practice and
experience shall give them that confidence, elegance and precision which
alone can make the accomplishment graceful and profitable.

"Advice to Youth," *Mark Twain: Collected Tales, Sketches, Speeches, & Essays, 1852–1890*, p. 802.
Library of America (1992). Speech, April 15, 1882, to Saturday Morning Club, Boston.

I should never come across a "proof" which wasn't thin and cheap and
probably had a fraud like me behind it.

The Autobiography of Mark Twain, ch. 11, p. 61. Harper & Row (1959).

Often, the surest way to convey misinformation is to tell the strict truth.

Following the Equator, ch. 59 (1897).

Carlyle said "a lie cannot live." It shows that he did not know how to tell
them. If I had taken out a life policy on this one the premiums would have
bankrupted me ages ago.

Mark Twain's Own Autobiography, ch. 9, ed. Michael J. Kiskis, University of Wisconsin Press (1990).
First published in the *North American Review*, vol. 184, no. 606 (January 4, 1907).

Do not tell fish stories where the people know you; but particularly, don't
tell them where they know the fish.

"More Maxims of Mark," *Mark Twain: Collected Tales, Sketches, Speeches, & Essays, 1891–1910*, p. 942.
Library of America (1992).

DECISIONS

It was a close place. I took it up, and held it in my hand. I was trembling, because I'd got to decide, forever, betwixt two things, and I knowed it. I studied a minute, sort of holding my breath, and then says to myself: "All right, then, I'll go to hell"—and tore it up.

Huck, in *Adventures of Huckleberry Finn*, ch. 31 (1885).

DEMOCRACY

A little citizenship ought to be taught at the mother's knee and in the nursery. Citizenship is what makes a republic; monarchies can get along without it. What keeps a republic on its legs is good citizenship.

"Layman's Sermon," *Mark Twain's Speeches*, p. 281. Gabriel Wells (1923). Speech, March 4, 1906.

I am a democrat only on principle, not by instinct—nobody is *that*. Doubtless some people *say* they are, but this world is grievously given to lying.

Notebook, ch. 31, ed. Albert Bigelow Paine (1935). Entry Feb.–March 1898.

DENTISTS

The dentist who talks well—other things being equal—is the one to choose. He tells anecdotes all the while and keeps his man so interested and entertained that he hardly notices the flight of time.

"Down the Rhine," *Europe and Elsewhere*, p. 162. Gabriel Wells (1923). Written in 1891.

DESIRE

To promise not to do a thing is the surest way in the world to make a body want to go and do that very thing.

The Adventures of Tom Sawyer, ch. 22, p. 211. Harper & Brothers (1903). Written in 1876.

A human being has a natural desire to have more of a good thing than he needs.

> *Following the Equator*, vol. 1, ch. 14, p. 132. Gabriel Wells (1923). Written in 1897.

DESPAIR

It is a time when one's spirit is subdued and sad, one knows not why; when the past seems a storm-swept desolation, life a vanity and a burden, and the future but a way to death.

> *The Gilded Age*, ch. 60 (1873). Referring to Laura Hawkins's mood.

DETERMINATION

As a final instance of the force of limitations in the development of concentration, I must mention that beautiful creature, Helen Keller, whom I have known for these many years. I am filled with wonder of her knowledge, acquired because shut out from all distraction. If I could have been deaf, dumb, and blind I also might have arrived at something.

> "Woman's Press Club," *Mark Twain's Speeches*, p. 100. Harper & Brothers (1910).

DIARIES

If you wish to inflict a heartless and malignant punishment upon a young person, pledge him to keep a journal a year.

> *The Innocents Abroad*, vol. 1, ch. 4, p. 26. Gabriel Wells (1923). Written in 1869.

DIFFERENCE

People are different. And it is the best way.

> "Tom Sawyer, Detective," *Tom Sawyer Abroad: Tom Sawyer, Detective, and Other Stories*, ch. 2, p. 122. Harper & Brothers (1910). Written in 1896.

*D*IPLOMATS

They want to send me abroad, as a Consul or a Minister. I said I didn't want any of the pie. God knows I am mean enough and lazy enough, now, without being a foreign consul.

Mark Twain's Letters, vol. 2, p. 179. University of California (1990). Letter to Jane Clemens, Twain's mother; dated February 6, 1868.

*D*ISAPPOINTMENT

A man has no business to be depressed by a disappointment, anyway; he ought to make up his mind to get even.

A Connecticut Yankee in King Arthur's Court, ch. 22, p. 200. Gabriel Wells (1923). Written in 1889 .

*D*ISCONTENT

There isn't a Parallel of Latitude but thinks it would have been the Equator if it had its rights.

"Pudd'nhead Wilson's New Calendar," *Following the Equator*, vol. 2, ch. 33, p. 366. Gabriel Wells (1923). Written in 1897.

*D*ISCOVERY

What is there that confers the noblest delight? What is that which swells a man's breast with pride above that which any other experience can bring to him? Discovery! To know that you are walking where none others have walked; that you are beholding what human eye has not seen before; that you are breathing a virgin atmosphere. To give birth to an idea, to discover a great thought—an intellectual nugget, right under the dust of a field that many a brain-plough had gone over before. To find a new planet, to invent a new hinge, to find a way to make the lightnings carry your messages. To be the *first*—that is the idea.

The Innocents Abroad, ch. 26 (1869).

October 12, the Discovery. It was wonderful to find America, but it would have been more wonderful to miss it.

Pudd'nhead Wilson and Those Extraordinary Twins, conclusion (1894).

DISSENT

The citizen who thinks he sees that the commonwealth's political clothes are worn out, and yet holds his peace and does not agitate for a new suit, is disloyal; he is a traitor.

A Connecticut Yankee in King Arthur's Court, ch. 13, p. 107. Gabriel Wells (1923). Written in 1889 .

The rule is perfect: *in all matters of opinion our adversaries are insane.*

Christian Science, bk. 1, ch. 5 (1907), repr. in *What Is Man?* ed. Paul Baender (1973).

Ours is the "land of the free"—nobody denies that—nobody challenges it. (Maybe it is because we won't let other people testify.)

Roughing It, vol. 2, ch. 13, pp. 128-9. Harper & Brothers (1899). Written in 1872.

DOCTORS

He had had much experience of physicians, and said, "the only way to keep your health is to eat what you don't want, drink what you don't like, and do what you'd druther not."

Following the Equator, ch. 49, Gabriel Wells (1923). Written in 1897.

How welcome is the face of the doctor, in that time of uncertainty when you can't tell for sure just where you are going to.

Mark Twain's Notebook, p. 218. Harper & Brothers (1935). Written about 1891.

DOGS

Heaven goes by favor. If it went by merit, you would stay out and your dog would go in.

Quoted in *Mark Twain: A Biography* (Paine), vol. 3, p. 1567. Gabriel Wells (1923).

If you pick up a starving dog and make him prosperous, he will not bite you. This is the principal difference between a dog and a man.

"Pudd'nhead Wilson's Calendar," *Pudd'nhead Wilson*, ch. 16 (1894).

DRAMA

I am killing only one man in this tragedy now, and that is bad, for nothing helps out a play like bloodshed. But in a few days I propose to introduce the smallpox into the last act. And if that don't work I shall close with a general massacre.

"Curtain Speech," *Mark Twain Speaking*, p. 88. University of Iowa Press, 1976. Addressing the audience at the opening of his play, *The Gilded Age*, September 16, 1874.

DREAMS

One sees nothing in a dream which is original in shape.

Mark Twain's Notebooks and Journals, vol. 3, p. 43. University of California (1979). Written Spring 1883-September 1884.

DRUNKENNESS

He had enough liquor there for two drunks and one delirium tremens.

Adventures of Huckleberry Finn, ch. 6, p. 39. Gabriel Wells (1923). Written in 1885.

DUELLING

I thoroughly disapprove of duels. I consider them unwise and I know they are dangerous. Also, sinful. If a man should challenge me now I would go to that man and take him kindly and forgivingly by the hand and lead him to a quite retired spot and *kill* him.

The Autobiography of Mark Twain, ch. 23, p. 129. Harper & Row (1959).

Much as the modern French duel is ridiculed by certain smart people, it is in reality one of the most dangerous institutions of our day. Since it is always fought in the open air the combatants are nearly sure to catch cold.

A Tramp Abroad, vol. 1, ch. 8, p. 62. Harper & Brothers (1899). Written in 1880.

DUTY

Make it a point to do something every day that you don't want to do. This is the golden rule for acquiring the habit of doing your duty without pain.

"Pudd'nhead Wilson's New Calendar," *Following the Equator*, vol. 2, ch. 22, p. 230. Gabriel Wells (1923). Written in 1897.

Duties are not performed for duty's *sake*, but because their *neglect* would make the man *uncomfortable*. A man performs but *one* duty—the duty of contenting his spirit, the duty of making himself agreeable to himself.

Old Man, in "What Is Man?" sct. 2 (1906), repr. in *Complete Essays*, ed. Charles Neider (1963).

EARTHQUAKES

We know of nothing that will answer as a substitute for one of those convulsions—to an unmarried man.

"No Earthquake," *Early Tales and Sketches*, vol. 2, p. 458. University of California (1981). Referring to earthquakes. First appeared August 23, 1864.

EDITORS

How often we recall, with regret, that Napoleon once shot at a magazine editor and missed him and killed a publisher. But we remember with charity that his intentions were good.

Mark Twain's Letters, p. 800. Gabriel Wells (1923). Letter to Henry Alden, November 1906.

$\mathcal{E}$DUCATION

After supper she got out her book and learned me about Moses and the Bulrushers; and I was in a sweat to find out all about him; but by and by she let it out that Moses had been dead a considerable long time; so then I didn't care no more about him; because I don't take no stock in dead people.

Huck, in *Adventures of Huckleberry Finn*, ch. 1 (1885).

All schools, all colleges, have two great functions; to confer, and to conceal, valuable knowledge. The theological knowledge which they conceal cannot justly be regarded as less valuable than that which they reveal. That is, when a man is buying a basket of strawberries it can profit him to know that the bottom half of it is rotten.

"More Maxims of Mark," *Mark Twain: Collected Tales, Sketches, Speeches, & Essays, 1891–1910*, p. 941, Library of America (1992).

When I am king, they shall not have bread and shelter only, but also teaching out of books; for a full belly is little worth where the mind is starved.

The Prince and the Pauper, ch. 4, p. 23. Harper & Brothers (1881). Written in 1882.

Training is everything. The peach was once a bitter almond; cauliflower is nothing but cabbage with a college education.

Pudd'nhead Wilson and Those Extraordinary Twins, ch. 5 (1894).

He ketched a frog one day and took him home and said he cal'lated to educate him; and so he never done nothing for three months but set in his back yard and learn that frog to jump. And you bet he *did* learn him, too. He'd give him a little punch behind, and the next minute you'd see that frog whirling in the air like a doughnut—see him turn one summerset, or maybe a couple, if he got a good start, and come down flat-footed and all right, like a cat. . . . Smiley said all a frog wanted was education, and he could do most anything—and I believe him.

Simon Wheeler, in "The Notorious Jumping Frog of Calaveras County," *Mark Twain: Collected Tales, Sketches, Speeches, & Essays, 1852–1890*, p. 592. Library of America (1992).

Efficiency

You may say organize, organize, organize; but there may be so much organization that it will interfere with the work to be done.

"Municipal Corruption," *Mark Twain's Speeches*, p. 218. Gabriel Wells (1923). Speech, January 4, 1901.

Egotism

It's like a cat pretending to be a cataract.

Mark Twain's Notebooks and Journals, vol. 3, p. 450. University of California (1979). Written July 1888–May 1889.

Elevators

The cigar-box which the European calls a "lift" needs but to be compared with our elevators to be appreciated. The lift stops to reflect between floors. That is all right in a hearse, but not in elevators. The American elevator acts like the man's patent purge—it works.

"Municipal Government," *Mark Twain's Speeches*, ed. William Dean Howells, Harpers (1910). Speech, December 6, 1900, to the St. Nicholas Society, New York.

Embarrassment

Man is the only animal that blushes. Or needs to.

"Pudd'nhead Wilson's New Calendar," *Following the Equator*, ch. 27 (1897).

Emotion

That is the way we are made: we don't reason, where we feel; we just feel.

A Connecticut Yankee in King Arthur's Court, ch. 11, p. 88. Gabriel Wells (1923). Written in 1889.

All emotion is involuntary when genuine.

"Cooper's Prose Style," *Letters from the Earth*, p. 142. Harper & Row (1962).

EMPIRES

We *must* annex those people. We can afflict them with our wise and beneficent government. We can introduce the novelty of thieves, all the way up from street-car pickpockets to municipal robbers and Government defaulters, and show them how amusing it is to arrest them and try them and then turn them loose—some for cash and some for "political influence." We can make them ashamed of their simple and primitive justice. . . . We can make that little bunch of sleepy islands the hottest corner on earth, and array it in the moral splendor of our high and holy civilization. Annexation is what the poor islanders need. "Shall we to men benighted, the lamp of life deny?"

"The Sandwich Islands," (1866), repr. in *Complete Essays,* ed. Charles Neider (1963).

ENJOYMENT

A good and wholesome thing is a little harmless fun in this world; it tones a body up and keeps him human and prevents him from souring.

Joan of Arc, bk. 2, ch. 21, p. 200. Harper & Brothers (1881). Written in 1896.

ENVY

Few of us can stand prosperity. Another man's, I mean.

"Pudd'nhead Wilson's New Calendar," *Following the Equator,* vol. 2, ch. 4, p. 38. Gabriel Wells (1923). Written in 1897.

Man will do many things to get himself loved, he will do all things to get himself envied.

"Pudd'nhead Wilson's New Calendar," *Following the Equator,* ch. 21 (1897).

EQUALITY

No civilization can be perfect until exact equality between man and woman is included.

Mark Twain's Notebook, p. 256 . Harper & Brothers (1935). Written about 1895.

*E*SCAPES

I reckon I got to light out for the Territory ahead of the rest, because Aunt Sally she's going to adopt me and sivilize me and I can't stand it. I been there before.

Huck, in *The Adventures of Huckleberry Finn*, ch. 43 (1885).

Huck waited for no particulars. He sprang away and sped down the hill as fast as his legs could carry him.

The Adventures of Tom Sawyer, ch. 29 (1876).

*E*TIQUETTE

When you got to the table you couldn't go right to eating, but you had to wait for the widow to tuck down her head and grumble a little over the victuals, though there warn't really anything the matter with them.

Huck, in *Adventures of Huckleberry Finn*, ch. 1 (1885).

*E*VIL

Every one is a moon, and has a dark side which he never shows to anybody.

"Pudd'nhead Wilson's New Calendar," *Following the Equator*, vol. 2, ch. 30, p. 327. Gabriel Wells (1923). Written in 1897.

*E*VOLUTION

Evolution is the law of policies: Darwin said it, Socrates endorsed it, Cuvier proved it and established it for all time in his paper on "The Survival of the Fittest." These are illustrious names, this is a mighty doctrine: nothing can ever remove it from its firm base, nothing dissolve it, but evolution.

"Three Thousand Years Among the Microbes," ch. 8, *Which Was the Dream?*, Ed. John S. Tuckey (1967).

EXAGGERATION

In my enthusiasm I may have exaggerated the details a little, but you will easily forgive me that fault, since I believe it is the first time I have ever deflected from perpendicular fact.

"Dinner Speech," *Mark Twain Speaking*, p. 114. University of Iowa Press (1976). Speech, December 17, 1877.

EXAMPLES

Few things are harder to put up with than the annoyance of a good example.

"Pudd'nhead Wilson's Calendar," *Pudd'nhead Wilson*, ch. 1 (1894).

EXCUSES

The girl who was rebuked for having borne an illegitimate child, excused herself by saying, "But it is such a *little* one."

"To My Missionary Critics," *Europe and Elsewhere* , p. 285. Gabriel Wells (1923). Written in April 1901.

EXERCISE

I have never taken any exercise, except sleeping and resting, and I never intend to take any. Exercise is loathsome. And it cannot be any benefit when you are tired; and I was always tired.

"Seventieth Birthday Speech," *Mark Twain: Collected Tales, Sketches, Speeches, & Essays, 1891–1910*, p. 716. Library of America (1992).

EXPERIENCE

Experience, the only logic sure to convince a diseased imagination and restore it to rugged health.

The American Claimant, ch. 23, p. 203. Harper & Brothers, 1896. Written in 1892.

It was only just words, words,—they meant nothing in the world to him, I might just as well have whistled. Words realize nothing, vivify nothing to you, unless you have suffered in your own person the thing which the words try to describe.

> Hank Morgan, in *A Connecticut Yankee in King Arthur's Court*, ch. 28 (1889).

Travel is fatal to prejudice, bigotry, and narrow-mindedness, and many of our people need it sorely on these accounts. Broad, wholesome, charitable views of men and things cannot be acquired by vegetating in one little corner of the earth all one's lifetime.

> *The Innocents Abroad*, vol. 2, "Conclusion," p. 407. Gabriel Wells (1923). Written in 1869.

We should be careful to get out of an experience only the wisdom that is in it—and stop there; lest we be like the cat that sits down on a hot stove-lid. She will never sit down on a hot stove-lid again—and that is well; but also she will never sit down on a cold one anymore.

> "Pudd'nhead Wilson's New Calendar," *Following the Equator*, ch. 11 (1897).

There is nothing that saps one's confidence as the knowing how to do a thing.

> "Remarks," *Mark Twain Speaking*, p. 434. University of Iowa Press (1976). Speech, May 30, 1902.

As by the fires of experience, so by commission of crime, you learn real morals. Commit all the crimes, familiarize yourself with all sins, take them in rotation (there are only two or three thousand of them), stick to it, commit two or three every day, and by-and-by you will be proof against them. When you are through you will be proof against all sins and morally perfect. You will be vaccinated against every possible commission of them. This is the only way.

> "Theoretical and Practical Morals," *Mark Twain's Speeches*, p. 132. Harper & Brothers (1910).

Expertise

No, the romance and the beauty were all gone from the river. All the value any feature of it had for me now was the amount of usefulness it could furnish toward compassing the safe piloting of a steamboat. Since those days, I have pitied doctors from my heart. What does the lovely flush in a beauty's cheek mean to a doctor but a "break" that ripples above some deadly disease? Are not all her visible charms sown thick with what are to him the signs and symbols of hidden decay? Does he ever see her beauty at all, or doesn't he simply view her professionally, and comment upon her unwholesome condition all to himself? And doesn't he sometimes wonder whether he has gained most or lost most by learning his trade?

Life on the Mississippi, ch. 9 (1883). Originally published as "Old Times on the Mississippi," *Atlantic Monthly* (1874).

Facts

Always dress a fact in tights, never in an ulster.

Life on the Mississippi, ch. 44 (1883). Originally published as "Old Times on the Mississippi," *Atlantic Monthly* (1874).

Faith

There are those who scoff at the schoolboy, calling him frivolous and shallow. Yet it was the schoolboy who said "Faith is believing what you know ain't so."

Following the Equator, ch. 12 (1897).

Fame

Tom was a glittering hero once more—the pet of the old, the envy of the young. His name even went into immortal print, for the village paper magnified him. There were some that believed he would be President, yet, if he escaped hanging.

The Adventures of Tom Sawyer, ch. 24 (1876).

What a hero Tom was become now! He did not go skipping and prancing, but moved with a dignified swagger as became a pirate who felt that the public eye was on him.

The Adventures of Tom Sawyer, ch. 18 (1876).

FANTASY

To be human is to have one's little modicum of romance secreted away in one's composition. One never ceases to make a hero of one's self (in private).

The Gilded Age, vol. 1, ch. 10, p. 118. Harper & Brothers (1901). Written in 1873.

FATHERS

My father and I were always on the most distant terms when I was a boy—a sort of armed neutrality, so to speak. At irregular intervals this neutrality was broken, and suffering ensued; but I will be candid enough to say that the breaking and the suffering were always divided up with strict impartiality between us—which is to say, my father did the breaking, and I did the suffering.

"A Memory," *Mark Twain: Collected Tales, Sketches, Speeches, & Essays, 1852–1890*, p. 428. Library of America (1992).

FEELINGS

My heart got to thumping. You can't reason with your heart; it has its own laws, and thumps about things which the intellect scorns.

Hank Morgan, in *A Connecticut Yankee in King Arthur's Court*, ch. 20 (1889).

FIDGETING

If you are with quality, or at a funeral, or trying to go to sleep when you ain't sleepy—if you are anywheres where it won't do for you to scratch, why you will itch all over in upward of a thousand places.

Adventures of Huckleberry Finn, ch. 2, p. 6. Gabriel Wells (1923). Written in 1885.

*F*LATTERY

She had more sand in her than any girl I ever see: in my opinion she was just full of sand. It sounds like flattery, but it ain't no flattery.

Huck, in *Adventures of Huckleberry Finn*, ch. 28 (1885).

*F*OOLS *AND* FOLLIES

Hain't we got all the fools in town on our side? and ain't that a big enough majority in any town?

The king, in *Adventures of Huckleberry Finn*, ch. 26 (1885).

Damndest fool; you know, he'd go and try to warm himself by a hotel register.

Mark Twain's Notebooks and Journals, vol. 3, p. 242. University of California (1979). Written March 1886–June 1887.

April 1. This is the day upon which we are reminded of what we are on the other three hundred and sixty-four.

"Pudd'nhead Wilson's Calendar," *Pudd'nhead Wilson*, ch. 21, p. 186. Gabriel Wells (1923). Written in 1894.

Let us be thankful for the fools. But for them the rest of us could not succeed.

"Pudd'nhead Wilson's New Calendar," *Following the Equator*, ch. 28 (1897).

*F*OREIGN *COUNTRIES*

The gentle reader will never, never know what a consummate ass he can become, until he goes abroad.

The Innocents Abroad, ch. 23 (1869).

FOREIGN POLICY

The principle of give and take—give one and take ten—the principle of diplomacy.

"The Dinner to Mr. Choate," *Mark Twain's Speeches*, p. 243. Gabriel Wells (1923). Speech, November 24, 1901.

FOREIGNERS

They spell it Vinci and pronounce it Vinchy; foreigners always spell better than they pronounce.

The Innocents Abroad, ch. 19 (1869).

FORGETFULNESS

A person's memory has no more sense than his conscience and no appreciation whatever of values and proportions.

The Autobiography of Mark Twain, ch. 11, pp. 54-6. Harper & Row (1959).

FORGIVENESS

If we should deal out justice only, in this world, who would escape? No, it is better to be generous, and in the end more profitable, for it gains gratitude for us, and love.

The Autobiography of Mark Twain, vol. 1, p. 189. Gabriel Wells (1925).

FORTUNE

It seems to be a law of the human condition that those that deserve shall not have and those that do not deserve shall get everything that is worth having.

The Autobiography of Mark Twain, ch. 60, p. 318. Harper & Row (1959).

FOUNTAIN-PEN, THE

None of us can have as many virtues as the fountain-pen, or half its cussedness; but we can try.

"Pudd'nhead Wilson's New Calendar," *Following the Equator*, vol. 2, ch. 32, p. 354. Gabriel Wells (1923). Written in 1897.

FOURTH OF JULY, THE

July 4. Statistics show that we lose more fools on this day than in all other days of the year put together. This proves, by the number left in stock, that one Fourth of July per year is now inadequate, the country has grown so.

"Pudd'nhead Wilson's Calendar," *Pudd'nhead Wilson*, ch. 17, p. 147. Gabriel Wells (1923). Written in 1894.

FRANCE AND THE FRENCH

No country offers greater security to life and property than France, and one has all the freedom he wants, but no license—no license to interfere with anybody, or make any one uncomfortable.

The Innocents Abroad, vol. 1, ch. 13, p. 123. Gabriel Wells (1923). Written in 1869.

They say there is no word for "home" in the French language. Well, considering they have the article itself in such an attractive aspect, they ought to manage to get along without the word.

The Innocents Abroad, vol. 1, ch. 12, p. 98. Gabriel Wells (1923). Written in 1869.

France has neither winter nor summer nor morals—apart from these drawbacks it is a fine country.

Mark Twain's Notebooks and Journals, entry in notebook 18, vol. 2, ed. Frederick Anderson (1975).

FREEDOM

We said there warn't no home like a raft, after all. Other places do seem so cramped up and smothery, but a raft don't. You feel mighty free and easy and comfortable on a raft.

Huck, in *The Adventures of Huckleberry Finn*, ch. 18 (1885).

FREEDOM OF SPEECH

It is by the goodness of God that in our country we have those three unspeakably precious things: freedom of speech, freedom of conscience, and the prudence never to practice either of them.

Following the Equator, ch. 20 (1897).

FRIENDS AND FRIENDSHIP

The holy passion of friendship is of so sweet and steady and loyal and enduring a nature that it will last through a whole lifetime, if not asked to lend money.

"Pudd'nhead Wilson's Calendar," *Pudd'nhead Wilson,* ch. 8 (1894).

FUNERALS

Where a blood relation sobs, an intimate friend should choke up, a distant acquaintance should sigh, a stranger should merely fumble sympathetically with his handkerchief.

"From an Unfinished Burlesque of Books on Etiquette," pt. 1, "At the Funeral," *Letters from the Earth,* ed. Bernard DeVoto (1962).

Twain added: "Where the occasion is military, the emotions should be graded according to military rank, the highest officer present taking precedence in emotional violence, and the rest modifying their feelings according to their position in the service."

In order to know a community, one must observe the style of its funerals and know what manner of men they bury with most ceremony.

Roughing It, vol. 2, ch. 47, p. 59. Harper & Brothers (1899). Written in 1872.

FUTILITY ✗✗✗✗ !!

He is useless on top of the ground; he ought to be be under it, inspiring the cabbages.

"Pudd'nhead Wilson's Calendar," *Pudd'nhead Wilson,* ch. 21 (1894).

GENIUS

Thousands of geniuses live and die undiscovered—either by themselves or by others.

Autobiography, ch. 27, ed. Charles Neider (1959).

Hunger is the handmaid of genius.

"Pudd'nhead Wilson's New Calendar," *Following the Equator,* vol. 2, ch. 7, p. 64. Gabriel Wells (1923). Written in 1897.

GENTLEMEN

If any man has just merciful and kindly instincts he would be a gentleman.

"Layman's Sermon," *Mark Twain's Speeches,* p. 283. Gabriel Wells (1923). Speech, March 4, 1906.

GERMANY AND THE GERMANS

Whenever the literary German dives into a sentence, that is the last you are going to see of him till he emerges on the other side of his Atlantic with his verb in his mouth.

A Connecticut Yankee in King Arthur's Court, ch. 22 (1889).

I can *understand* German as well as the maniac that invented it, but I *talk* it best through an interpreter.

Quoted in "German," *Greatly Exaggerated,* ed. Alex Ayres (1988).

Twain described German as "the language which enables a man to travel all day in one sentence without changing cars."

Never knew before what Eternity was made for. It is to give some of us a chance to learn some German.

> Mark Twain's Notebooks and Journals, vol. 2, p. 121. University of California, 1975. Written July–August 1878.

GOD

God's inhumanity to man makes countless thousands mourn.

> Mark Twain's Notebook, ed. Albert B. Paine (1935).

Who gave his angels eternal happiness unearned, yet required his other children to earn it.

> "The Mysterious Stranger," The Portable Mark Twain, ch. 11, p. 743. Viking, 1946. Referring to God. Written 1897–1908.

GOLF

Golf is a good walk spoiled.

> Quoted in "Golf," Greatly Exaggerated, ed. Alex Ayres (1988).

GOODNESS

What's the use you learning to do right when it's troublesome to do right and ain't no trouble to do wrong, and the wages is just the same.

> Huck, in Adventures of Huckleberry Finn, ch. 16, p. 128. Gabriel Wells (1923).

To be good is noble; but to show others how to be good is nobler and no trouble.

> Following the Equator, preface (1897).

Always do right. This will gratify some people, and astonish the rest.

> Mark Twain in Eruption, frontispiece, ed. Bernard DeVoto, Harper (1940). Note, February 16, 1901, to Young People's Society, Brooklyn.

It is more trouble to make a maxim than it is to do right.

"Pudd'nhead Wilson's New Calendar," *Following the Equator*, vol. 1, ch. 3, p. 27. Gabriel Wells (1923). Written in 1897.

Let us endeavor so to live that when we die even the undertaker will be sorry.

"Pudd'nhead Wilson's Calendar," *Pudd'nhead Wilson*, ch. 6, p. 44. Gabriel Wells (1923). Written in 1894.

GOSSIP

It takes your enemy and your friend, working together, to hurt you to the heart: the one to slander you and the other to get the news to you.

"Pudd'nhead Wilson's New Calendar," *Following the Equator,* ch. 9 (1897)

GRAMMAR

Perfect grammar—persistent, continuous, sustained—is the fourth dimension, so to speak; many have sought it, but none has found it.

The Autobiography of Mark Twain, vol. 1, p. 173. Gabriel Wells (1925).

GRATITUDE

Gratitude and treachery are merely the two extremities of the same procession. You have seen all of it that is worth staying for when the band and the gaudy officials have gone by.

"Pudd'nhead Wilson's Calendar," *Pudd'nhead Wilson*, ch. 18, p. 150. Gabriel Wells (1923). Written in 1894.

GREED

The motto ["In God We Trust"] stated a lie. If this nation ever trusted in God, that time has gone by; for nearly half a century almost its entire trust has been in the Republican party and the dollar—mainly the dollar.

"Andrew Carnegie," *Mark Twain in Eruption*, p. 50. Harper & Brothers (1940). Dictated in December, 1907.

Him? Grasping? Insatiable? That man wouldn't be satisfied if he had the contract to furnish hell with fuel.

Mark Twain's Notebooks and Journals, vol. 3, p. 250. University of California (1979). Thought to be a reference to John Wannemaker, the famous Philadelphia merchant. Written March 1886–June 1887.

GROWTH

What is the most rigorous law of our being? Growth. No smallest atom of our moral, mental, or physical structure can stand still a year. It grows—it must grow; nothing can prevent it.

"Consistency," paper, read in Hartford, Connecticut, 1884, repr. in *Complete Essays*, ed. Charles Neider (1963).

GUILT

An uneasy conscience is a hair in the mouth.

Mark Twain's Notebook, p. 392 . Harper & Brothers (1935). Written about 1904.

Near by is an interesting ruin—the meagre remains of an ancient heathen temple—a place where human sacrifices were offered up in those old bygone days when the simple child of nature, yielding momentarily to sin when sorely tempted, acknowledged his error when calm reflection had shown it to him, and came forward with noble frankness and offered up his grandmother as an atoning sacrifice—in those old days when the luckless sinner could keep on cleansing his conscience and achieving periodical happiness as long as his relations held out.

Roughing It, ch. 64, American Publishing Company (1871).

GULLIBILITY

How easy it is to make people believe a lie and how hard it is to undo that work again!

The Autobiography of Mark Twain, ch. 11, p. 61. Harper & Row (1959).

GUNFIGHTING

And the next instant . . . he was one of the deadest men that ever lived.

Roughing It, vol. 1, ch. 10, p. 87. Harper & Brothers (1899). Referring to one of the victims of the outlaw Slade. First appeared in 1872.

HABITS

Old habit of mind is one of the toughest things to get away from in the world. It transmits itself like physical form and feature.

A Connecticut Yankee in King Arthur's Court, ch. 22, p. 201. Gabriel Wells (1923). Written in 1889 .

Habit is habit, and not to be flung out of the window by any man, but coaxed downstairs a step at a time.

"Pudd'nhead Wilson's Calendar," Pudd'nhead Wilson, ch. 6 (1894).

I have stopped smoking now and then, for a few months at a time, but it was not on principle, it was only to show off; it was to pulverize those critics who said I was a slave to my habits and couldn't break my bonds.

"Seventieth Birthday Speech," Mark Twain: Collected Tales, Sketches, Speeches, & Essays, 1891–1910, pp. 715–16. Library of America (1992).

HABITS, BAD

Now I don't approve of dissipation, and I don't indulge in it, either, but I haven't a particle of confidence in a man who has no redeeming petty vices.

"Answers to Correspondents,"Early Tales and Sketches, vol. 2, p. 190. University of California (1981). Written in June 1865.

In my early manhood and in middle life I used to vex myself with reforms every now and then. And I never had occasion to regret these divergencies for, whether the resulting deprivations were long or short, the rewarding pleasure which I got out of the vice when I returned to it always paid me for all that it cost.

The Autobiography of Mark Twain, vol. 2, p. 102. Gabriel Wells (1925).

A man may have no bad habits and have worse.

"Pudd'nhead Wilson's New Calendar," *Following the Equator*, vol. 1, ch. 1, p. 1. Gabriel Wells (1923). Written in 1897.

$\mathcal{H}$ABITS, GOOD

There are three things that you should never do on any occasion. First, girls, don't smoke—that is, don't smoke to excess. I am seventy-three and one half years old, and have been smoking seventy-three of them. But I never smoke to excess—that is, I smoke in moderation, only one cigar at a time. Second, don't drink–that is don't drink to excess. Third, don't marry—I mean, to excess.

"Remarks," *Mark Twain Speaking*, p. 645. University of Iowa Press (1976). Speech, June 9, 1909.

Rise early—it is the early bird that catches the worm. Don't be fooled by this absurd saw. I once knew a man who tried it. He got up at sunrise and a horse bit him.

Mark Twain's Notebooks and Journals, vol. 1, p. 184. University of California, 1975. Written March–April 1866.

$\mathcal{H}$APPINESS

Happiness ain't a *thing in itself*—it's only a *contrast* with something that ain't pleasant. . . . And so, as soon as the novelty is over and the force of the contrast dulled, it ain't happiness any longer, and you have to get something fresh.

Sam Bartlett, in *Captain Stormfield's Visit to Heaven*, ch. 1 (written 1907). Published in *The Complete Short Stories*, ed. Charles Neider (1957).

Wrinkles should merely indicate where smiles have been.

Following the Equator, ch. 52 (1897).

Good friends, good books and a sleepy conscience: this is the ideal life.

"More Maxims of Mark," *Mark Twain: Collected Tales, Sketches, Speeches, & Essays, 1891–1910*, p. 943, Library of America (1992).

Are you so unobservant as not to have found out that sanity and happiness are an impossible combination?

"The Mysterious Stranger," *The Portable Mark Twain*, ch. 10, p. 735. Viking, 1946. Written 1897-1908.

There are people who can do all fine and heroic things but one: keep from telling their happinesses to the unhappy.

"Pudd'nhead Wilson's New Calendar," *Following the Equator*, ch. 26 (1897).

*H*ATE

A strange and vanity-devoured, detestable woman! I do not believe I could ever learn to like her except on a raft at sea with no other provisions in sight.

The Autobiography of Mark Twain, ch. 76, ed. Charles Neider, Harper & Row (1959).

*H*EALTH

It seems a pity that the world should throw away so many good things merely because they are unwholesome. I doubt if God has given us any refreshment which, taken in moderation, is unwholesome, except microbes. Yet there are people who strictly deprive themselves of each and every eatable, drinkable and smokeable which has in any way acquired a shady reputation. They pay this price for health. And health is all they get for it. How strange it is! It is like paying out your whole fortune for a cow that has gone dry.

The Autobiography of Mark Twain, vol. 1, p. 98. Gabriel Wells (1925).

To have nothing the matter with you and no habits is pretty tame, pretty colorless. It is just the way a saint feels, I reckon; it is at least the way he looks. I never could stand a saint.

"Marienbad—Health Factory," *Europe and Elsewhere*, p. 119. Gabriel Wells (1923). Written February 7, 1892.

HEART, THE

It is in the heart that the values lie. I wish I could make him understand that a loving good heart is riches, and riches enough, and that without it intellect is poverty.

"Eve's Diary," *Collected Tales, Sketches, and Essays: 1891-1910*, p. 700. Library of America (1992). Eve, referring to Adam. First appeared in December 1905.

HEAVEN

I begin to see that a man's got to be in his own heaven to be happy.

Eli Stormfield, in "Extracts from Capt. Stormfield's Visit to Heaven," *Mark Twain: Collected Tales, Sketches, Speeches, & Essays, 1891–1910, p. 835*. Library of America (1992).

Heaven for climate, hell for company.

Mark Twain's Notebooks and Journals, vol. 3, p. 538. University of California (1979). Written May 1889–August 1890.

HELL

When I think of some of our shipments to it I realize that I should feel more or less at home there. It wouldn't surprise me there to recognize our American twang here and there.

"Bishop Speech," *Mark Twain Speaking*, p. 592. University of Iowa Press (1976). Referring to hell. Speech, October 1907.

HEROES

One can be a hero to other folk, and in a sort of vague way understand it, or at least believe it, but that a person can really be a hero to a near and familiar friend is a thing which no hero has ever yet been able to realize.

The *Autobiography of Mark Twain*, ch. 16, p. 89. Harper & Row (1959).

HISTORY

The very ink in which history is written is merely fluid prejudice.

"Pudd'nhead Wilson's New Calendar," *Following the Equator,* ch. 69 (1897).

HOMELINESS

A thoroughly beautiful woman and a perfectly homely woman are creations which I love to gaze upon, and which I cannot tire of gazing upon, for each is perfect in her own line, and it is *perfection*, I think, in many things, and perhaps most things, which is the quality that fascinates us.

The *Autobiography of Mark Twain*, vol. 1, pp. 323-4. Gabriel Wells (1925).

HONESTY

It is not worth while to strain one's self to tell the truth to people who habitually discount everything you tell them, whether it is true or isn't.

The *Autobiography of Mark Twain*, ch. 12, p. 67. Harper & Row (1959).

Whenever I have diverged from custom and principle and uttered a truth, the rule has been that the hearer hadn't strength enough to believe it.

The *Autobiography of Mark Twain*, ch. 26, p. 143. Harper & Row (1959).

One's conscience can never be the worse for the knowledge that he has paid his way like a man.

> *The Innocents Abroad*, vol. 2, ch. 23, p. 265. Gabriel Wells (1923). Written in 1869.

Tell the truth or trump—but get the trick.

> "Pudd'nhead Wilson's Calendar," *Pudd'nhead Wilson*, ch. 1, p. 1. Gabriel Wells (1923). Written in 1894.

Truth is stranger than fiction—to some people, but I am measurably familiar with it.

> "Pudd'nhead Wilson's New Calendar," *Following the Equator*, vol. 1, ch. 15, p. 137. Gabriel Wells (1923). Written in 1897.

When in doubt, tell the truth.

> "Pudd'nhead Wilson's New Calendar," *Following the Equator*, vol. 1, ch. 2, p. 12. Gabriel Wells (1923). Written in 1897.

HOPE

For a little while, hope made a show of reviving—not with any reason to back it, but only because it is in its nature to revive when the spring has not been taken out of it by age and familiarity with failure.

> *The Adventures of Tom Sawyer*, ch. 31, p. 288. Harper & Brothers (1903). Written in 1876.

HORSES

I have known the horse in war and in peace, and there is no place where a horse is comfortable. The horse has too many caprices, and he is too much given to initiative. He invents too many ideas. No, I don't want anything to do with a horse.

> "Welcome Home," *Mark Twain's Speeches*, p. 201. Gabriel Wells (1923). Written November 10, 1900.

HOTELS

It used to be good hotel, but that proves nothing—I used to be a good boy.

> *The Innocents Abroad*, vol. 2, ch. 27, p. 366. Gabriel Wells (1923). Written in 1869.

It is an art apart. Saint Francis of Assisi said—"All saints can do miracles, but few of them can keep hotel."

Mark Twain's Notebook, ed. Albert B. Paine (1935).

$\mathcal{H}$UMAN NATURE

It is my conviction that the human race is no proper target for harsh words and bitter criticisms, and that the only justifiable feeling toward it is compassion; it did not invent itself, and it had nothing to do with the planning of its weak and foolish character.

The Autobiography of Mark Twain, ch. 63, p. 337. Harper & Row (1959).

Of all the animals, man is the only one that is cruel. He is the only one that inflicts pain for the pleasure of doing it.

"Man's Place in the Animal World," *What Is Man? and Other Philosophical Writings*, p. 84. University of California (1973). Written about 1896.

Human nature cannot be studied in cities except at a disadvantage—a village is the place. There you can know your man inside and out—in a city you but know his crust; and his crust is usually a lie.

Mark Twain's Notebooks and Journals, vol. 2, p. 503. University of California, 1975. Written January 1882–February 1883.

$\mathcal{H}$UMAN RACE, THE

Such is the human race. Often it does seem such a pity that Noah and his party did not miss the boat.

Christian Science, bk. 2, ch. 7 (1907), repr. in *What Is Man?*, ed. Paul Baender (1973).

I have no race prejudices, and I think I have no color prejudices or caste prejudices nor creed prejudices. Indeed I know it. I can stand any society. All that I care to know is that a man is a human being—that is enough for me; he can't be any worse.

"Concerning the Jews," *The Man that Corrupted Hadleyburg and Other Stories and Essays*, p. 254. Harper & Brothers (1900). Written in October 1899.

Man was made at the end of the week's work, when God was tired.

Mark Twain's Notebook, p. 381. Harper & Brothers (1935). Written about 1903.

*H*UMOR

The humorous story depends for its effect upon the *manner* of the telling.

"How to Tell a Story," *The Man that Corrupted Hadleyburg and Other Stories and Essays*, p. 225. Harper & Brothers (1900). Written in 1895.

The funniest things are the forbidden.

Mark Twain's Notebooks and Journals, vol. 2, p. 304. University of California, 1975. Written February–September 1879.

There is no difference between Wit and humor, except that Wit can succeed without any pretense of being unconscious, but humor can't.

Mark Twain's Notebooks and Journals, vol. 3, pp. 449-50. University of California (1979). Written July 1888–May 1889.

Wit is the sudden marriage of ideas which before their union were not perceived to have any relation.

Mark Twain's Notebooks and Journals, vol. 3, p. 172. University of California (1979). Written April–August 1885.

Against the assault of laughter nothing can stand.

"The Mysterious Stranger," *The Portable Mark Twain*, ch. 10, p. 737. Viking, 1946. Written 1897–1908.

Everything human is pathetic. The secret source of Humor itself is not joy but sorrow. There is no humor in heaven.

"Pudd'nhead Wilson's New Calendar," *Following the Equator*, vol. 1, ch. 10, p. 101. Gabriel Wells (1923). Written in 1897.

*H*UNGER

The cayote is a living, breathing allegory of Want. He is *always* hungry. He is always poor, out of luck and friendless. The meanest creatures despise him, and even the fleas would desert him for a velocipede.

Roughing It, ch. 5, American Publishing Company (1871).

Hypocrisy

We all went to church, about three mile, everybody a-horseback. The men took their guns along, so did Buck, and kept them between their knees or stood them handy against the wall. The Shepherdson's done the same. It was pretty ornery preaching—all about brotherly love, and such-like tiresomeness; but everybody said it was a good sermon, and they all talked it over going home, and had such a powerful lot to say about faith, and good works, and free grace, and preforeordestination, and I don't know what all, that it did seem to me to be one of the roughest Sundays I had run across yet.

Huck, in *The Adventures of Huckleberry Finn*, ch. 18 (1885).

It is not best that we use our morals week days; it gets them out of repair for Sundays.

Mark Twain's Notebook, p. 345. Harper & Brothers (1935). Written about 1898.

Ignorance

In religion and politics people's beliefs and convictions are in almost every case gotten at second-hand, and without examination, from authorities who have not themselves examined the questions at issue but have taken them at second hand from other non-examiners, whose opinions about them were not worth a brass farthing.

The Autobiography of Mark Twain, ch. 78, p. 401. Harper & Row (1959).

If you had made the acquiring of ignorance the study of your life, you could not have graduated with higher honor than you could to-day.

The regular editor, in "How I Edited an Agricultural Newspaper," pp. 415–16, *Mark Twain: Collected Tales, Sketches, Speeches, & Essays, 1852–1890*, Library of America (1992).

I was gratified to be able to answer promptly, and I did. I said I didn't know.

Life on the Mississippi, ch. 6 (1883).

ILLUSION

To be human is to have one's little modicum of romance secreted away in one's composition. One never ceases to make a hero of one's self, (in private,) during life, but only alters the style of heroism from time to time as the drifting years belittle certain gods of his admiration and raise up others in their stead.

The Gilded Age, ch. 10 (1873).

Don't part with your illusions. When they are gone you may still exist, but you have ceased to live.

"Pudd'nhead Wilson's New Calendar," *Following the Equator*, ch. 59 (1897).

It isn't safe to sit in judgment upon another person's illusion when you are not on the inside. While you are thinking it is a dream, he may be knowing it is a planet.

"Three Thousand Years Among the Microbes," *Which Was the Dream?* ch. 13, ed. John S. Tuckey (1967).

IMAGINATION

No doubt it's a blessed thing to have an imagination that can always make you satisfied, no matter how you are fixed.

Mrs. Sellers, in *The American Claimant* (1892).

Their very imagination was dead. When you can say that of a man, he has struck bottom, I reckon; there is no lower deep for him.

Hank Morgan, in *A Connecticut Yankee in King Arthur's Court*, ch. 20 (1889).

Imagination labors best in distant fields.

The Innocents Abroad, vol. 2, ch. 23, p. 262. Gabriel Wells (1923). Written in 1869.

IMPERIALISM

Soap and education are not as sudden as a massacre, but they are more deadly in the long run.

"Facts Concerning the Recent Resignation," *Sketches New and Old*, p. 350. Harper & Brothers (1903). Written in February 1868.

All the territorial possessions of all the political establishments in the earth—including America, of course—consist of pilferings from other people's wash.

Following the Equator (1897).

I have traveled more than any one else, and I have noticed that even the angels speak English with an accent.

"Pudd'nhead Wilson's New Calendar," *Following the Equator*, vol. 2, "Conclusion", p. 379. Gabriel Wells (1923). Written in 1897.

Shall we go on conferring our Civilization upon these peoples that sit in darkness, or shall we give those poor things a rest?

"To the Person Sitting in Darkness," *Europe and Elsewhere*, p. 255. Gabriel Wells (1923). Written in February 1901.

IMPULSIVENESS

We are all creatures of sudden impulse. We must be worked up by steam.

"Votes for Women," *Mark Twain's Speeches*, p. 222. Gabriel Wells (1923). Written January 20, 1901.

INDECISION

I must have a prodigious quantity of mind; it takes me as much as a week, sometimes, to make it up.

The Innocents Abroad, ch. 7 (1869).

INDEPENDENCE

A pilot, in those days, was the only unfettered and entirely independent human being that lived in the earth. Kings are but the hampered servants of parliament and people; parliaments sit in chains forged by their constituency; the editor of a newspaper cannot be independent, but must work with one hand tied behind him by party and patrons, and be content to utter only half or two thirds of his mind; no clergyman is a free man and may speak the truth regardless of his parish's opinions; writers of all kinds are manacled servants of the public. We write frankly and fearlessly, but then we "modify" before we print. In truth, every man and woman and child has a master, and worries and frets in servitude; but in the day I write of, the Mississippi pilot had *none*.

Life on the Mississippi, ch. 14 (1883). Originally published as "Old Times on the Mississippi," *Atlantic Monthly* (1874).

INDUSTRY

Diligence is a grand thing, but taking things easy is much more—restful.

"Business," *Mark Twain's Speeches*, pp. 235-6. Gabriel Wells (1923). Speech, March 30, 1901.

INEQUALITY

I have a religion—but you will call it blasphemy. It is that there is a God for the rich man but none for the poor.

Mark Twain's Letters, vol. 1, p. 324. University of California (1988). Letter, dated October 20, 1865, to Orion and Mollie Clemens, Twain's brother and sister-in-law.

INEXPERIENCE

Don't you know, there are some things that can beat smartness and foresight? Awkwardness and stupidity can. The best swordsman in the world doesn't need to fear the second best swordsman in the world; no, the person for him to be afraid of is some ignorant antagonist who has never had a sword in his hand before; he doesn't do the thing he ought to.

A Connecticut Yankee in King Arthur's Court, ch. 34, p. 344. Gabriel Wells (1923). Written in 1889 .

INHERITANCE

It is good to begin life poor; it is good to begin life rich—these are wholesome; but to begin it poor and *prospectively* rich! The man who has not experienced it cannot imagine the curse of it.

The Autobiography of Mark Twain, ch. 6, p. 27. Harper & Row (1959).

INSANITY

Let us consider that we are all partially insane. It will explain us to each other; it will unriddle many riddles; it will make clear and simple many things which are involved in haunting and harassing difficulties and obscurities now.

Christian Science, bk. 1, ch. 5 (1907), repr. in *What Is Man?*, ed. Paul Baender (1973).

The way it is now, the asylums can hold the sane people, but if we tried to shut up the insane we should run out of building materials.

Following the Equator, vol. 2, ch. 14, p. 155. Gabriel Wells (1923). Written in 1897.

INSANITY PLEA, THE

Of late years it does not seem possible for a man to so conduct himself, before killing another man, as not to be manifestly insane. If he talks about the stars, he is insane. If he appears nervous and uneasy an hour before the killing, he is insane. If he weeps over a great grief, his friends shake their heads, and fear that he is "not right." If, an hour after the murder, he seems ill at ease, preoccupied and excited, he is unquestionably insane. Really, what we want now, is not laws against crime, but a law against *insanity*.

"A New Crime," *Sketches Old and New*, p. 250. Harper & Brothers (1903). Written in 1870.

*I*NSECTS

As a thinker and planner the ant is the equal of any savage race of men; as a self-educated specialist in several arts she is the superior of any savage race of men; and in one or two high mental qualities she is above the reach of any man, savage or civilized!

The Old Man, in "What Is Man?" Sect. 6 (1906), repr. in *Complete Essays*, ed. Charles Neider (1963).

*I*NSPIRATION

A book is pretty sure to get tired along about the middle and refuse to go on with its work until its powers and its interests should have been refreshed by a rest and its depleted stock of raw materials reinforced by lapse of time.

The Autobiography of Mark Twain, ch. 53, p. 288. Harper & Row (1959).

I made the great discovery that when the tanks runs dry you've only to leave it alone and it will fill up again in time, while you are asleep—also while you are work on other things and are quite unaware that this unconscious and profitable cerebration is going on.

The Autobiography of Mark Twain (Neider), ch. 53, p. 289. Harper & Row (1959).

*I*NSTITUTIONS

Monarchies, aristocracies, and religions are all based upon that large defect in your race—the individual's distrust of his neighbor, and his desire, for safety's or comfort's sake, to stand well in his neighbor's eye. These institutions will always remain, and always flourish, and always oppress you, affront you, and degrade you, because you will always be and remain slaves of minorities. There was never a country where the majority of the people were in their secret hearts loyal to any of these institutions.

Satan, in "The Mysterious Stranger," ch. 9 (1916).

INSULT

If a person offends you, and you are in doubt as to whether it was intentional or not, do not resort to extreme measures; simply watch your chance and hit him with a brick.

"Advice to Youth," *Mark Twain's Speeches,* p. 104. Gabriel Wells (1923). Written about 1882.

Human beings feel dishonor the most, sometimes, when they most deserve it.

The Autobiography of Mark Twain, ch. 11, p. 58. Harper & Row (1959).

INTELLECT

A man's brain (intellect) is stored powder; it cannot touch itself off; the fire must come from the outside.

Mark Twain's Notebook, p. 365. Harper & Brothers (1935). Written about 1898.

INTELLECTUALS

You've got to admire men that deal in ideas of that size and can tote them around without crutches.

Life on the Mississippi, ch. 28 (1883). Originally published as "Old Times on the Mississippi," *Atlantic Monthly* (1874).

INTOLERANCE

If a man doesn't believe as we do, we say he is a crank, and that settles it. I mean it does nowadays, because now we can't burn him.

Following the Equator, vol. 2, ch. 17, p. 193. Gabriel Wells (1923). Written in 1897.

He is the only animal that loves his neighbor as himself, and cuts his throat if his theology isn't straight.

"Man's Place in the Animal World," *What Is Man? and Other Philosophical Writings*, p. 85. University of California (1973). Written about 1896.

*I*RREVERENCE

Irreverence is the champion of liberty and its only sure defense.

Mark Twain's Notebook, p. 195. Harper & Brothers (1935). Written about 1888.

True irreverence is disrespect for another man's god.

"Pudd'nhead Wilson's New Calendar," *Following the Equator*, ch. 53 (1897).

*I*TALY AND THE ITALIANS

Lump the whole thing! Say that the Creator made Italy from designs by Michael Angelo!

Dan, in *The Innocents Abroad*, ch. 27 (1896).

Twain's surfeit of and exasperation with Michelangelo during his visit to Rome was eloquently expressed: "I used to worship the mighty genius of Michael Angelo. . . . But I do not want Michael Angelo for breakfast—for luncheon—for dinner—for tea—for supper—for between meals. . . . Here—here it is frightful. He designed St Peter's; he designed the Pope. . . the eternal bore designed the Eternal City, and unless all men and books do lie, he painted everything in it!. . . I never felt so fervently thankful, so soothed, so tranquil, so filled with the blessed peace, as I did yesterday when I learned that Michael Angelo was dead."

*J*EWELRY

Let us not be too particular. It is better to have old second-hand diamonds than none at all.

"Pudd'nhead Wilson's New Calendar," *Following the Equator*, ch. 34 (1897).

*J*OKES

The only way to classify the majestic ages of some of those jokes was by geologic periods.

A Connecticut Yankee in King Arthur's Court, ch. 4, p. 30. Gabriel Wells (1923). Written in 1889.

There isn't such thing as a new joke possible.

A Connecticut Yankee in King Arthur's Court, ch. 4, p. 30. Gabriel Wells (1923). Written in 1889.

*J*OURNALISTS AND JOURNALISM

News is history in its first and best form, its vivid and fascinating form, and history is the pale and tranquil reflection of it.

The Autobiography of Mark Twain, vol. 1, p. 326. Gabriel Wells (1925).

All conscientious scruples—all generous feelings must give way to our inexorable duty—which is to keep the public mind in a healthy state of excitement, and experience has taught us that blood alone can do this.

"A Duel Prevented," *Early Tales and Sketches*, vol. 1, pp. 265-6. University of California (1979). Published August 2, 1863.

Nothing in the world affords a newspaper reporter so much satisfaction as gathering up the details of a bloody and mysterious murder.

"The Killing of Julius Caesar 'Localized,'" *Sketches Old and New*, p. 385. Harper & Brothers (1903). Published 1864.

It seems to me that just in the ration that our newspapers increase, our morals decay.

"License of the Press," *Mark Twain's Speeches*, p. 47. Gabriel Wells (1923).

That awful power, the public opinion of a nation, is created in America by a horde of ignorant, self-complacent simpletons who failed at ditching and shoemaking and fetched up in journalism on their way to the poorhouse.

"License of the Press," *Mark Twain's Speeches*, p. 49. Gabriel Wells (1923). Written in 1873.

If a spectacle is going to be particularly imposing I prefer to see it through somebody else's eyes, because that man will always exaggerate. Then I can exaggerate his exaggeration, and my account of the thing will be the most impressive.

"O'Shah," *Europe and Elsewhere*, p. 53. Gabriel Wells (1923). Written in July 1878.

Reporting is the best school in the world to get a knowledge of human beings, human nature, and human ways.

"Roughing It," *Mark Twain Speaking*, p. 60. University of Iowa Press, 1976. Speech, December 1871.

There are only two forces that can carry light to all the corners of the globe ... the sun in the heavens and the Associated Press down here.

"Spelling and Pictures," *Mark Twain's Speeches,* ed. Albert Bigelow Paine (1923). Speech, September 18, 1906, to Associated Press, New York City.

Look at the mother of Washington! She raised a boy that could not tell a lie—could not tell a lie! But he never had any chance. It might have been different if he had belonged to the Washington Newspaper Correspondents' Club.

"Woman—An Opinion," *Mark Twain's Speeches,* p. 32. Gabriel Wells (1923).

JUDGMENT

You can't depend on your judgment when your imagination is out of focus.

Mark Twain's Notebook, p. 344. Harper & Brothers (1935). Written about 1897.

JURIES

We have a criminal jury system which is superior to any in the world; and its efficiency is only marred by the difficulty of finding twelve men every day who don't know anything and can't read.

"After-Dinner Speech," *Sketches Old and New,* p. 235. Harper & Brothers (1903). Speech, July 4, 1873.

KILLING

If the desire to kill and the opportunity to kill came always together, who would escape hanging?

Following the Equator, ch. 46 (1897).

KNOWLEDGE

I believe that whenever a human being, of even the highest intelligence and culture, delivers an opinion upon a matter apart from his particular and especial line of interest, training and experience, it will always be an opinion of so foolish and so valueless a sort that it can be depended upon to suggest to our Heavenly Father that the human being is another disappointment and that he is no considerable improvement upon the monkey.

The Autobiography of Mark Twain, ch. 57, p. 304. Harper & Row (1959).

We have not the reverent feeling for the rainbow that a savage has, because we know how it is made. We have lost as much as we gained by prying into that matter.

A Tramp Abroad, vol. 2, ch. 11 (1879).

LABOR

I do not like work even when another person does it.

"The Lost Napoleon," *Europe and Elsewhere*, p. 172. Gabriel Wells (1923). Written in 1901.

LANGUAGE

He had not failed to observe how harmoniously gigantic language and a microscopic topic go together.

"A Cat Tale," p. 770, *Mark Twain: Collected Tales, Sketches, Speeches, & Essays, 1852–1890*, Library of America (1992).

LAUGHTER

Such a laugh was money in a man's pocket, because it cut down on the doctor's bills like everything.

The Adventures of Tom Sawyer, ch. 30, p. 276. Harper & Brothers (1903). Written in 1876.

[Humanity] has unquestionably one really effective weapon—laughter. Power, money, persuasion, supplication, persecution—these can lift at a colossal humbug—push it a little—weaken it a little, century by century; but only laughter can blow it to rags and atoms at a blast. Against the assault of laughter nothing can stand.

Satan, in *The Mysterious Stranger*, ch. 10 (1916).

*L*AW

It grieves me to think how far more profound and reverent a respect the law would have for literature if a body could only get drunk on it.

"Dinner Speech in Montreal," *Mark Twain: Collected Tales, Sketches, Speeches, & Essays, 1852–1890*, p. 777. Library of America (1992). Discussing the lack of international copyright law.

To succeed in the other trades, capacity must be shown; in the law, concealment of it will do.

Following the Equator, ch. 37 (1897).

*L*AZINESS

From the beginning of my sojourn in this world there was a persistent vacancy in me where the industry ought to be.

The Autobiography of Mark Twain (Neider), ch. 30, p. 166. Harper & Row (1959).

I have often noticed that you shun exertion. There comes the difference between us. I court exertion. I love work. Why, sir, when I have a piece of work to perform, I go away to myself, sit down in the shade and muse over the coming enjoyment.

Mark Twain's Letters, vol. 1, p. 92. University of California (1988). Letter, dated July 6, 1859, to John Moore, a friend from Twain's days on the river. .

LEARNING

We could use up two eternities in learning all that is to be learned about our own world and the thousands of nations that have risen and flourished and vanished from it. Mathematics alone would occupy me 8 million years.

Mark Twain's Notebooks and Journals, vol. 3, p. 56. University of California (1979). Written Spring 1883–September 1884.

LIBERTY

In *truth*, the surest way for a man to make of himself a target for almost universal scorn, obloquy, slander, and insult is to stop twaddling about these priceless independencies, and attempt to *exercise* one of them.

"Consistency," *Mark Twain's Speeches*, p. 125. Gabriel Wells (1923). Referring to freedoms of conscience, opinion, speech, and action, 1884.

LIES AND LYING

When a person cannot deceive himself the chances are against his being able to deceive other people.

The Autobiography of Mark Twain, ch. 36, p. 204. Harper & Row (1959).

It may be that this girl had a fact in her somewhere but I don't believe you could have sluiced it out with a hydraulic.

A Connecticut Yankee in King Arthur's Court, ch. 11, p. 87. Gabriel Wells (1923). Written in 1889.

The only difference that I know of between a silent lie and a spoken one is, that the silent lie is a less respectable one than the other. And it can deceive, whereas the other can't.

Following the Equator, vol. 2, ch. 3, p. 29. Gabriel Wells (1923). Written in 1897.

It is often the case that the man who can't tell a lie thinks he is the best judge of one.

"Pudd'nhead Wilson's Calendar," *Pudd'nhead Wilson*, "Conclusion," p. 201. Gabriel Wells (1923). Written in 1894.

Often, the surest way to convey misinformation is to tell the strictest truth.

"Pudd'nhead Wilson's New Calendar," *Following the Equator*, vol. 2, ch. 23, p. 246. Gabriel Wells (1923). Written in 1897.

One of the most striking differences between a cat and a lie is that a cat only has nine lives.

"Pudd'nhead Wilson's Calendar," *Pudd'nhead Wilson*, ch. 7, p. 51. Gabriel Wells (1923). Written in 1894.

There are eight hundred and sixty-nine different forms of lying, but only one of them has been squarely forbidden. Thou shalt not bear false witness against they neighbor.

"Pudd'nhead Wilson's New Calendar," *Following the Equator*, vol. 2, ch. 19, p. 205. Gabriel Wells (1923). Written in 1897.

LIFE

Why is it that we rejoice at a birth and grieve at a funeral? It is because we are not the person involved.

"Pudd'nhead Wilson's Calendar," *Pudd'nhead Wilson*, ch. 9, p. 69. Gabriel Wells (1923). Written in 1894.

LITERATURE

I don't know anything that mars good literature so completely as too much truth.

"The Savage Club Dinner," *Mark Twain's Speeches*, p. 354. Gabriel Wells (1923). Speech, July 6, 1907.

LONELINESS

By and by it got sort of lonesome, and so I went and set on the bank and listened to the current swashing along, and counted the stars and drift-logs and rafts that come down, and then went to bed; there ain't no better way to put in time when you are lonesome.

Huck, in *Adventures of Huckleberry Finn*, ch. 8, p. 54. Gabriel Wells (1923). First appeared in 1885.

There is no God, no universe, no human race, no earthly life, no heaven, no hell. It is all a dream, a grotesque and foolish dream. Nothing exists but you. And you are but a *thought*—a vagrant thought, a useless thought, a homeless thought, wandering forlorn among the empty eternities!

Satan's last words to Theodor Fischer, in *The Mysterious Stranger*, ch. 11 (1916), repr. in *The Complete Short Stories*, ed. Charles Neider (1957).

*L*OSS

Nothing that grieves us can be called little: by the eternal laws of proportion a child's loss of a doll and a king's loss of a crown are events of the same size.

"Which Was the Dream?" (Written 1897), published in *Which Was the Dream and Other Symbolic Writings,* ed. John S. Tuckey (1967).

*L*OVE

Love seems the swiftest, but it is the slowest of all growths. No man or woman really knows what perfect love is until they have been married a quarter of a century.

Mark Twain's Notebook, p. 235 . Harper & Brothers (1935). Written about 1894.

When you fish for love, bait with your heart, not your brain.

Mark Twain's Notebook, p. 346. Harper & Brothers (1935). Written about 1898.

Love is a madness; if thwarted it develops fast.

"The Memorable Assassination," *What Is Man? and Other Essays*, p. 171. Harper & Brothers, 1917. Written about 1898.

*M*ADNESS

When we remember that we are all mad, the mysteries disappear and life stands explained.

Mark Twain's Notebook, p. 345. Harper & Brothers (1935). Written about 1898.

No sane man can be happy, for to him life is real, and he sees what a fearful thing it is.

> Satan, in *The Mysterious Stranger*, ch. 10 (1916).

MANNERS

The world loses a good deal by the laws of decorum; gains a good deal, of course, but certainly loses a good deal.

> *The Autobiography of Mark Twain*, ch. 42, p. 235. Harper & Row (1959).

Good breeding consists in concealing how much we think of ourselves and how little we think of the other person.

> *Mark Twain's Notebook*, p. 345. Harper & Brothers (1935). Written about 1898.

The highest perfection of politeness is only a beautiful edifice, built, from the base to the dome, of ungraceful and gilded forms of charitable and unselfish lying.

> "On the Decay of the Art of Lying," (written 1882), published in *The Complete Humorous Sketches and Tales of Mark Twain*, ed. Charles Neider (1961).

MARRIAGE

People talk about beautiful friendships between two persons of the same sex. What is the best of that sort, compared with the friendship of man and wife, where the best impulses and highest ideals of both are the same? There is no place for comparison between the two friendships; the one is earthly, the other divine.

> *A Connecticut Yankee in King Arthur's Court*, ch. 42, p. 409. Gabriel Wells (1923). Written in 1889.

"A good wife would be a perpetual incentive to progress"—and so she would—I never thought of that before—progress from house to house because I couldn't pay the rent.

> *Mark Twain's Letters*, vol. 2, p. 133. University of California (1990). Letter, dated December 12, 1867, to Mary Fairbanks, a friend from the *Quaker City* cruise.

$\mathcal{M}$ARTYRDOM

Martyrdom covers a multitude of sins.

Notebook, ch. 33, entry for May 23, 1903, ed. Albert Bigelow Paine (1935).

$\mathcal{M}$ASSES, THE

The master minds of all nations, in all ages, have sprung in affluent multitude from the mass of the nation, and from the mass of the nation only—not from its privileged classes.

A Connecticut Yankee in King Arthur's Court, ch. 15 (1889).

$\mathcal{M}$ASTURBATION

Michelangelo said to Pope Julius II, "Self negation is noble, self-culture is beneficent, self-possession is manly, but to the truly great and inspiring soul they are poor and tame compared to self-abuse." Mr. Brown, here, in one of his latest and most graceful poems refers to it in an eloquent line which is destined to live to the end of time—"None know it but to love it, None name it but to praise."

"Some Thoughts on the Science of Onanism," *Mark Twain: Collected Tales, Sketches, Speeches, & Essays, 1852–1890*, p. 722. Library of America (1992).

Of all the various kinds of sexual intercourse, this has the least to recommend it. As an amusement it is too fleeting; as an occupation it is too wearing; as a public exhibition there is no money in it.

"Some Thoughts on the Science of Onanism," *Mark Twain Speaking*, p. 126. University of Iowa Press, 1976. Referring to masturbation, Spring 1879.

$\mathcal{M}$ATERIALISM

Any so-called material thing that you want is merely a symbol: you want it not for *itself*, but because it will content your spirit for the moment.

Old Man, in *What Is Man?* sct. 6 (1906), repr. in *Complete Essays*, ed. Charles Neider (1963).

*M*ATURITY

Genius has no youth, but starts with the ripeness of age and old experience.

Mark Twain: A Biography (Paine), vol. 2, p. 1089. Gabriel Wells (1923).

*M*AXIMS

Maxim-mongers are loathsome people.

Mark Twain's Notebooks and Journals, vol. 2, p. 482. University of California (1975). Written January 1882–February 1883.

*M*EANNESS

I think his heart was merely a pump and had no other function.

The Autobiography of Mark Twain, ch. 25, p. 137. Harper & Row (1959).

*M*ELANCHOLY

We have our graver moods; they come to us all; the lightest of us cannot escape them. These moods have their appetites—healthy and legitimate appetites—and there ought to be some way of satisfying them.

"The Man that Corrupted Hadleyburg," *The Man that Corrupted Hadleyburg and Other Stories and Essays*, p. 248. Harper & Brothers (1900). Written in December 1899.

*M*IND, THE

Life does not consist mainly—or even largely—of facts and happenings. It consists mainly of the storm of thoughts that is forever blowing through one's head.

The Autobiography of Mark Twain, vol. 1, p. 283. Gabriel Wells (1925).

What do you think of the human mind? I mean, in case you think there is a human mind.

Satan, in *Letters from the Earth*, p. 8 (1962).

MIRACLES

You can't throw too much style into a miracle. It costs trouble, and work, and sometimes money; but it pays in the end.

A Connecticut Yankee in King Arthur's Court, ch. 23, p. 213. Gabriel Wells (1923). Written in 1889 .

MISCHIEF

I see that every man that went in had his pockets bulging, or something muffled up under his coat—and I see it warn't no perfumery either, not by a long sight. I smelt sickly eggs by the barrel, and rotten cabbages, and such things; and if I know the signs of a dead cat being around, and I bet I do, there was sixty-four of them went in. I shoved in there for a minute, but it was too various for me, I couldn't stand it.

Huck, in *The Adventures of Huckleberry Finn*, ch. 23 (1885).

MISSIONARY WORK

O kind missionary, O compassionate missionary, leave China! Come home and convert these Christians!

"The United States of Lyncherdom," *A Pen Warmed-up in Hell*, p. 159. Harper & Row (1972). Written in 1901.

MODESTY

There's a breed of humility which is itself a species of showing-off.

"The Esquimau Maiden's Romance," *The Man that Corrupted Hadleyburg and Other Stories and Essays*, p. 202. Harper & Brothers (1900). Written in 1893.

The man who is ostentatious of his modesty is twin to the statue that wears a fig-leaf.

"Pudd'nhead Wilson's New Calendar," *Following the Equator,* ch. 50 (1897).

*M*ONEY

I went to the circus, and loafed around the back side till the watchman went by, and then dived in under the tent. I had my twenty-dollar gold piece and some other money, but I reckoned I better save it. . . . I ain't opposed to spending money on circuses, when there ain't no other way, but there ain't no use in *wasting* it on them.

Huck, in *The Adventures of Huckleberry Finn,* ch. 22 (1885).

The lack of money is the root of all evil.

"More Maxims of Mark," *Mark Twain: Collected Tales, Sketches, Speeches, & Essays, 1891–1910,* p. 944. Library of America (1992).

*M*ORALITY

It has always been a peculiarity of the human race that it keeps two sets of morals in stock—the private and real, and the public and artificial.

The Autobiography of Mark Twain, ch. 72, p. 377. Harper & Row (1959).

There are good *impulses,* there are evil impulses, and that is all. Half of the results of an good intention are evil; half the results of an evil intention are good. No man can command the result, nor allot them.

"The Dervish and the Offending Stranger," *Europe and Elsewhere,* p. 310. Gabriel Wells (1923). Written in 1902.

The low level which commercial morality has reached in America is deplorable. We have humble God fearing Christian men among us who will stoop to do things for a million dollars that they ought not to be willing to do for less than 2 millions.

"More Maxims of Mark," *Mark Twain: Collected Tales, Sketches, Speeches, & Essays, 1891–1910,* p. 944. Library of America (1992).

There is a Moral Sense, and there is an Immoral Sense. History shows us that the Moral Sense enables us to perceive morality and how to avoid it, and that the Immoral Sense enables us to perceive immorality and how to enjoy it.

"Pudd'nhead Wilson's New Calendar," *Following the Equator*, vol. 1, ch. 16, p. 143. Gabriel Wells (1923). Written in 1897.

As by the fires of experience, so by the commission of crimes, you learn real morals. Commit all the crimes, familiarize yourself with all sins, take them in rotation (there are only two or three thousand of them), stick to it. Commit two or three every day, and by and by you will be proof against them. When you are through you will be proof against all sins and morally perfect.

"Theoretical and Practical Morals," *Mark Twain's Speeches*, pp. 191-2. Gabriel Wells (1923). Speech, July 8, 1899.

If you grant that *one* man's conscience doesn't know right from wrong, it is an admission that there are others like it. This single admission pulls down the whole doctrine of infallibility of judgment in consciences.

"What Is Man?" *What Is Man? and Other Philosophical Writings*, p. 146. University of California (1973). Written in 1906.

$\mathcal{M}$ORALS

I'd rather teach them than practice them any day. "Give them to others"— that's my motto.

"Morals and Memory," *Mark Twain's Speeches*, pp. 284-5. Gabriel Wells (1923). Referring to morals, March 7, 1906.

The most permanent lessons in morals are those which come, not of booky teaching, but of experience.

A Tramp Abroad, vol. 2, ch. 18, p. 239. Harper & Brothers (1899). Written in 1880.

*M*OTIVES

From his cradle to his grave a man never does a single thing which has any FIRST AND FOREMOST object but one—to secure peace of mind, spiritual comfort, for HIMSELF.

Old Man, in "What Is Man?" sct. 2 (1906), repr. in *Complete Essays*, ed. Charles Neider (1963).

*M*URDER

All creatures kill—there seems to be no exception; but on the whole list, man is the only one that kills for fun; he is the only one that kills in malice, the only one that kills for revenge.

The Autobiography of Mark Twain, vol. 2, p. 7. Gabriel Wells (1925).

If the desire to kill and the opportunity to kill came always together, who would escape hanging?

"Pudd'nhead Wilson's New Calendar," *Following the Equator*, vol. 2, ch. 10, p. 98. Gabriel Wells (1923). Written in 1897.

*M*USIC AND MUSICIANS

Music *is* a good thing; and after all that soul-butter and hogwash, I never see it freshen up things so, and sound so honest and bully.

Huck, in *The Adventures of Huckleberry Finn*, ch. 25 (1885).

We often feel sad in the presence of music without words; and often more than that in the presence of music without music.

"More Maxims of Mark," *Mark Twain: Collected Tales, Sketches, Speeches, & Essays, 1891–1910*, p. 947. Library of America (1992).

A pretty air in an opera is prettier there than it could be anywhere else, I suppose, just as an honest man in politics shines more than he would elsewhere.

A Tramp Abroad, ch. 9 (1879).

We went to Mannheim and attended a shivaree—otherwise an opera—the one called "Lohengrin." The banging and slamming and booming and crashing were something beyond belief. The racking and pitiless pain of it remains stored up in my memory alongside the memory of the time that I had my teeth fixed.

A Tramp Abroad, ch. 9 (1879).

*N*ARRATIVE

There is this advantage about a story, anyway, that whatever moral or valuable thing you put into a speech, why, it gets diffused among those involuted sentences and possibly your audience goes away without finding out what that valuable thing was that you were trying to confer upon it; but, dear me, you put the same jewel into a story and it becomes the keystone of that story, and you are bound to get it—it flashes.

"Russian Sufferers," *Mark Twain's Speeches*, p. 264. Gabriel Wells (1923). Speech, December 18, 1905.

*N*ATIONALISM

Each nation *knowing* it has the only true religion and the only sane system of government, each despising all the others, each an ass and not suspecting it.

"What Is Man?" *What Is Man? and Other Philosophical Writings*, p. 213. University of California (1973). Written in 1906.

Nations do not *think*, they only *feel*. They get their feelings at second hand through their temperaments, not their brains. A nation can be brought by force of circumstances, not argument to reconcile itself to *any kind of government or religion that can be devised*; in time it will fit itself to the required conditions; later it will prefer them and will fiercely fight for them.

Old man, in *What Is Man?* sct. 6 (1906), repr. in *Complete Essays*, ed. Charles Neider (1963).

Necessity

Necessity knows no law.

The Innocents Abroad, vol. 2, ch. 24, p. 278. Gabriel Wells (1923). Written in 1869.

Ne'er-do-wells

He said he reckoned a body could reform the old man with a shotgun.

Adventures of Huckleberry Finn, ch. 5, p. 31. Gabriel Wells (1923). Huck reporting Judge Thatcher's opinion of Huck's pap. First appeared in 1885.

Nevada

The country looks something like a singed cat, owing to the scarcity of shrubbery, and also resembles that animal in the respect that it has more merits than its personal appearance would seem to indicate.

"Washoe—'Information Wanted,'" *Early Tales and Sketches*, vol. 1, p. 368. University of California (1979). Written in May 1864.

New England

I reverently believe that the Maker who made us all makes everything in New England but the weather. I don't know who makes that, but I think it must be raw apprentices in the weather-clerk's factory who experiment and learn how. . . . In the spring I have counted one hundred and thirty-six different kinds of weather inside of four-and-twenty hours.

"The Weather," *Mark Twain's Speeches*, ed. Albert Bigelow Paine (1923).

NEW YORK

I have at last, after several months' experience, made up my mind that [New York] is a splendid desert—a domed and steepled solitude, where the stranger is lonely in the midst of a million of his race.

Mark Twain's Travels with Mr. Brown, ch. 25, eds. Franklin Walker and G. Ezra Dane, Knopf (1940). Originally published in *Daily Alta California* (June 5, 1867).

In this absence of nine years I find a great improvement in the city of New York. . . . Some say it has improved because I have been away. Others, and I agree with them, say it has improved because I have come back.

Mark Twain's Speeches, ed. William Dean Howells, Harpers (1910). Speech, December 6, 1900, to the St. Nicholas Society, New York.

NEWSPAPERS

The first thing you want in new country, is a patent office; then work up your school system; and after that, out with your paper. A newspaper has its faults, and plenty of them, but no matter, it's hark from the tomb for a dead nation without it.

A Connecticut Yankee in King Arthur's Court, ch. 9, p. 70. Gabriel Wells (1923).

You try to tell *me* anything about the newspaper business! Sir, I have been through it from Alpha to Omaha, and I tell you that the less a man knows the bigger the noise he makes and the higher the salary he commands.

"How I Edited an Agricultural Paper" (1870).

The old saw says, "Let a sleeping dog lie." Still, when there is much at stake it is better to get a newspaper to do it.

"Pudd'nhead Wilson's New Calendar," *Following the Equator*, vol. 2, ch. 8, p. 75. Gabriel Wells (1923).

NIHILISM

Nietzsche published his book, and was at once pronounced crazy by the world—by a world which included tens of thousands of bright, sane men who believed exactly as Nietzsche believed, but concealed the fact, and scoffed at Nietzsche.

"Afterword: The Whole Human Race," *A Pen Warmed-up in Hell*, p. 176. Harper & Row (1972).

Nomadism

We are descended from desert-lounging Arabs, and countless ages of growth toward perfect civilization have failed to root out of us the nomadic instinct. We all confess to a gratified thrill at the thought of "camping-out."

Roughing It, vol. 1, ch. 27, p. 220. Harper & Brothers (1899). Written in 1872.

Nostalgia

School-boy days are no happier than the days of after life, but we look back upon them regretfully because we have forgotten our punishments.

The Innocents Abroad, vol. 2, ch. 27, p. 331. Gabriel Wells (1923). Written in 1869.

Novels

How much of his competency is derived from conscious "observation"? The amount is so slight that it counts for next to nothing in the equipment. Almost the whole capital of the novelists is the slow accumulation of *un*conscious observation—absorption.

"What Paul Bourget Thinks of Us," *How to Tell a Story and Other Essays*, p. 187. Harper & Brothers (1897). Written in 1895.

There is only one expert who is qualified to examine the souls and the life of a people and make a valuable report—the native novelist.

"What Paul Bourget Thinks of Us," *How to Tell a Story and Other Essays*, p. 186. Harper & Brothers (1897). Written in 1895.

Boston Public Library

Circulation system messages:
Patron status is ok.

Title: When in doubt, tell the truth : and other
quotations from Mark Twain
ID: 39999031037581
Due: 04/22/2019 23:59:59
Circulation system messages:
Item checkout ok.

Total items: 1
3/31/2019 4:51 PM
Checked out: 12
Overdue: 0
Hold requests: 0
Ready for pickup: 0

Circulation system messages:
The End Patron Message is OK

Thank you for using the
3M SelfCheck™ System.

OBEDIENCE

If your mother tells you to do a thing, it is wrong to reply that you won't. It is better and more becoming to intimate that you will do as she bids you, and then afterward act quietly in the matter according to the dictates of your better judgment.

"Advice for Good Little Girls,"*Early Tales and Sketches*, vol. 2, p. 244. University of California (1981). Written in 1865.

Always obey your parents, when they are present. This is the best policy in the long run, because if you don't they will make you. Most parents think they know better than you do, and you can generally make more by humoring that superstition than you can by acting on your own better judgment.

"Advice to Youth," *Mark Twain's Speeches*, p. 104. Gabriel Wells (1923). Written about 1882.

OLD AGE

Younger ones cannot know the full pathos that lies in those words—the lost opportunity; but anybody who is old, who has really lived and felt this life, he knows the pathos of the lost opportunity.

"Russian Sufferers," *Mark Twain's Speeches*, p. 265. Gabriel Wells (1923). Speech, December 18, 1905.

OLD TESTAMENT, THE

The two testaments are interesting, each in its own way. The Old gives us a picture of these people's Deity as he was before he got religion, the other one gives us a picture of him as he appeared afterward.

Letter 10, *Letters from the Earth*, p. 44. Harper & Row (1962). Written in 1909.

OPERAS

One in fifty of those who attend our operas likes it already, perhaps, but I think a good many of the other forty-nine go in order to be able to talk knowingly about it. The latter usually hum the airs while they are being sung, so that their neighbors may perceive that they have been to operas before. The funerals of these do not occur often enough.

A Tramp Abroad, vol. 1, ch. 9, p. 81. Harper & Brothers (1899). Written in 1880.

OPINION

Hardly a man in the world has an opinion upon morals, politics or religion which he got otherwise than through his associations and sympathies. Broadly speaking, there are none but corn-pone opinions. And broadly speaking, Corn-Pone stands for Self-Approval. Self-approval is acquired mainly from the approval of other people. The result is Conformity.

"Corn-Pone Opinions," (1923), repr. in What Is Man?, ed. Paul Baender (1973).

There is no place where people all think alike—well, there is heaven; there they do, but let us hope it won't always be so.

"Introducing Winston S. Churchill," Mark Twain Speaking, p. 367. University of Iowa Press (1976). Speech, December 12, 1900.

It were not best that we should all think alike; it is difference of opinion that makes horse-races.

"Pudd'nhead Wilson's Calendar," Pudd'nhead Wilson, ch. 19, p. 164. Gabriel Wells (1923). Written in 1894.

OPPORTUNITY

I was seldom able to see an opportunity until it ceased to be one.

The Autobiography of Mark Twain (Neider), ch. 44, p. 248. Harper & Row (1959).

OPPRESSION

A man *is* a man, at bottom. Whole ages of abuse and oppression cannot crush the manhood clear out of him. Whoever thinks it a mistake is mistaken himself. Yes, there is plenty good enough material for a republic in the most degraded people that ever existed.

> *A Connecticut Yankee in King Arthur's Court*, ch. 30, p. 301. Gabriel Wells (1923). Written in 1889.

ORIGINALITY

We have no thoughts of our own: they are transmitted to us, trained into us. All that is original in us, and therefore fairly creditable or discreditable to us, can be covered up and hidden by the point of a cambric needle, all the rest being atoms contributed by, and inherited from, a procession of ancestors that stretches back a billion years to the Adam-clam or grasshopper or monkey from whom our race has been so tediously and ostentatiously and unprofitably developed. And as for me, all that I think about in this plodding sad pilgrimage, this pathetic drift between the eternities, is to look out and humbly live a pure and high and blameless life, and save that one microscopic atom in me that is truly *me*: the rest may land in Sheol and welcome, for all I care.

> Hank Morgan, in *A Connecticut Yankee in King Arthur's Court*, ch. 18 (1889).

To do something, say something, see something, before *anybody* else—these are things that confer a pleasure compared with which other pleasures are tame and commonplace, other ecstacies cheap and trivial.

> *The Innocents Abroad*, ch. 26 (1869).

The man with a new idea is a crank until the idea succeeds.

> "Pudd'nhead Wilson's New Calendar," *Following the Equator,* ch. 32 (1897).

OUTLAWS

The true desperado is gifted with splendid courage, and yet he will take the most infamous advantage of his enemy; armed and free, he will stand up before a host and fight until he is shot all to pieces, and yet when he is under the gallows and helpless he will cry and plead like a child.

> *Roughing It*, vol. 1, ch. 11, p. 98. Harper & Brothers (1899). Written in 1872.

OVERWORK

What a robust people, what a nation of thinkers we might be, if we would lay ourselves on the shelf occasionally and renew our edges!

The Innocents Abroad, vol. 1, ch. 19, p. 184. Gabriel Wells (1923). Written in 1869.

PAIN

Do not undervalue the headache. While it is at its sharpest it seems a bad investment; but when relief begins, the unexpired remainder is worth $4 a minute.

"Pudd'nhead Wilson's New Calendar," *Following the Equator,* ch. 54 (1897).

PAINTING

Raphael was a bird. We had several of his chromos; one was his "Miraculous Draught of Fishes," where he puts in a miracle of his own— puts three men into a canoe which wouldn't have held a dog without upsetting. I always admired to study R.'s art, it was so fresh and unconventional.

A Connecticut Yankee in King Arthur's Court, ch. 6, p. 52. Gabriel Wells (1923). Written in 1889.

PARADES

A procession, to be valuable, must do one thing or the other—clothe itself in splendors and charm the eye, or symbolize something sublime and uplifting, and so appeal to the imagination.

"Queen Victoria's Jubilee," *Europe and Elsewhere*, p. 194. Gabriel Wells (1923).

*P*ARENTING

We are always too busy for our children; we never give them the time or interest they deserve. We lavish gifts upon them; but the most precious gift—our personal association, which means so much to them—we give grudgingly.

Quoted in *Mark Twain: A Biography* (Paine), vol. 3, p. 1299. Gabriel Wells (1923).

*P*ATENTS

A country without a patent office and good patent laws was just a crab, and couldn't travel any way but sideways or backways.

A Connecticut Yankee in King Arthur's Court, ch. 9, p. 68. Gabriel Wells (1923). Written in 1889 .

*P*ATIENCE

One thing at a time, is my motto—and just play that thing for all it is worth, even if it's only two pair and a jack.

A Connecticut Yankee in King Arthur's Court, ch. 2, p. 16. Gabriel Wells (1923). Written in 1889.

*P*ATRIOTISM

My kind of loyalty was loyalty to one's country, not to its institutions or its office-holders. The country is the real thing, the substantial thing, the eternal thing; it is the thing to watch over, and care for, and be loyal to; institutions are extraneous, they are its mere clothing, and clothing can wear out.

A Connecticut Yankee in King Arthur's Court, ch. 13, p. 107. Gabriel Wells (1923).

Patriot: The person who can holler the loudest without knowing what he is hollering about.

"More Maxims of Mark," *Mark Twain: Collected Tales, Sketches, Speeches, & Essays, 1891–1910*, p. 945. Library of America (1992).

In absolute monarchies it is furnished from the throne, cut and dried, to the subject; in England and America it is furnished, cut and dried, to the citizen by the politician and the newspaper.

"As Regards Patriotism," *Europe and Elsewhere*, p. 255. Gabriel Wells (1923). Referring to patriotism. Written about 1900.

I would throw out the old maxim, "My country, right or wrong," and instead I would say, "My country when she is right."

"Training That Pays," *Mark Twain Speaking*, p. 390. University of Iowa Press (1976). Speech, March 16, 1901.

PEACE

An inglorious peace is better than a dishonorable war.

"Glances at History," *A Pen Warmed-up in Hell*, p. 34. Harper & Row (1972).

PESSIMISM

There is no sadder sight than a young pessimist, except an old optimist.

Notebook, ch. 34, entry for December 27, 1903, ed. Albert Bigelow Paine (1935).

PITY

Pity is for the living, envy is for the dead.

"Pudd'nhead Wilson's New Calendar," *Following the Equator*, ch. 19 (1897).

PLAY

He had discovered a great law of human action, without knowing it—namely, that in order to make a man or a boy covet a thing, it is only necessary to make the thing difficult to attain. If he had been a great and wise philosopher, like the writer of this book, he would now have comprehended that Work consists of whatever a body is *obliged* to do and that Play consists of whatever a body is not obliged to do.

The Adventures of Tom Sawyer, ch. 2 (1876).

*P*LUMBERS

Thanksgiving Day. Let all give humble, hearty, and sincere thanks, now, but the turkeys. In the island of Fiji they do not use turkeys; they use plumbers. It does not become you and me to sneer at Fiji.

"Pudd'nhead Wilson's Calendar," *Pudd'nhead Wilson*, ch. 18, p. 150. Gabriel Wells (1923).

*P*OLICE

Let us abolish policemen who carry clubs and revolvers, and put in a squad of poets armed to the teeth with poems on spring and love.

"Dinner Speech," *Mark Twain Speaking*, p. 393. University of Iowa Press (1976). Speech, March 23, 1901.

*P*OLITICAL PARTIES

This atrocious doctrine of allegiance to *party* plays directly into the hands of politicians of the *baser* sort—and doubtless for *that* it was borrowed—or stolen—from the monarchical system.

"Consistency," Paper read at Hartford, Connecticut in 1884, repr. in *Complete Essays*, ed. Charles Neider (1963).

When the doctrine of allegiance to party can utterly up-end a man's moral constitution and make a temporary fool of him besides, what excuse are you going to offer for preaching it, teaching it, extending it, perpetuating it? Shall you say, the best good of the country demands allegiance to party? Shall you also say it demands that a man kick his truth and his conscience into the gutter, and become a mouthing lunatic, besides?

"Consistency," Paper read at Hartford, Connecticut in 1884, repr. in *Complete Essays*, ed. Charles Neider (1963).

$\mathcal{P}$OLITICS

I was an ardent Hayes man but that was natural, for I was young at the time. I have since convinced myself that the political opinions of a nation are of next to no value, in any case, but that what little rag of value they possess is to be found in the old, rather than among the young.

The Autobiography of Mark Twain, ch. 62, p. 331. Harper & Row (1959).

Party loyalty—a snare invented by designing men for selfish purposes.

The Autobiography of Mark Twain, vol. 2, p. 10. Gabriel Wells (1925).

To lodge all power in one party and keep it there is to insure bad government and the sure and gradual deterioration of the public morals.

The Autobiography of Mark Twain, vol. 2, p. 14. Gabriel Wells (1925).

A man must not hold himself aloof from the things which his friends and community have at heart if he would be liked—especially as a statesman.

A Connecticut Yankee in King Arthur's Court, ch. 9, p. 68. Gabriel Wells (1923). Written in 1889 .

Demagogue—a vessel containing beer and other liquids.

"Girls," p. 92, *Mark Twain's Speeches*, Harper & Brothers (1910).

$\mathcal{P}$ONY EXPRESS, THE

During the preceding night an ambushed savage had sent a bullet through the pony-rider's jacket, but he had ridden on, just the same, because pony-riders were not allowed to stop and inquire into such things unless killed.

Roughing It, vol. 1, ch. 9, p. 75. Harper & Brothers (1899). Written in 1872.

$\mathcal{P}$OPULARITY

By common consent of all the nations and all the ages the most valuable thing in this world is the homage of men, whether deserved or undeserved.

"At the Shrine of St. Wagner," (1891), repr. in *Complete Essays*, ed. Charles Neider (1963).

The best of us would rather be popular than right.

August Feldner, in *The Mysterious Stranger*, University of California Press (1969).

My books are water; those of the great geniuses are wine. Everybody drinks water.

Mark Twain's Notebooks and Journals, vol. 3, entry in Notebook 26, March 1886–June 1887, ed. Frederick Anderson (1979).

Even popularity can be overdone. In Rome, along at first, you are full of regrets that Michelangelo died; but by and by you only regret that you didn't see him do it.

"Pudd'nhead Wilson's Calendar," *Pudd'nhead Wilson*, ch. 17, p. 147. Gabriel Wells (1923). Written in 1894.

*P*OSTURING

The glory which is built upon a lie soon becomes a most unpleasant incumbrance.

The Autobiography of Mark Twain, ch. 11, p. 61. Harper & Row (1959).

*P*OVERTY AND THE POOR

Huck was always willing to take a hand in any enterprise that offered entertainment and required no capital, for he had a troublesome superabundance of that sort of time which is *not* money.

The Adventures of Tom Sawyer, ch. 25 (1876).

*P*OWER

Unlimited power *is* the ideal thing when it is in safe hands. The despotism of heaven is the one absolutely perfect government. An earthly despotism would be the absolutely perfect earthly government, if the conditions were the same, namely, the despot the perfectest individual of the human race, and his lease on life perpetual. But as perishable perfect man must die, and leave his despotism in the hands of an imperfect successor, an earthly despotism is mot merely a bad form of government, it is the worst form that is possible.

A Connecticut Yankee in King Arthur's Court, ch. 10, p. 77. Gabriel Wells (1923).

The Autocrat of Russia possesses more power than any other man in the earth; but he cannot stop a sneeze.

"Pudd'nhead Wilson's New Calendar," *Following the Equator,* vol. 1, ch. 35, p. 303. Gabriel Wells (1923). Written in 1897.

PRACTICAL JOKES

When a person of mature age perpetrates a practical joke it is fair evidence, I think, that he is weak in the head and hasn't enough heart to signify.

The Autobiography of Mark Twain, ch. 10, p. 54. Harper & Row (1959).

PRAISE

We are always more anxious to be distinguished for a talent which we do not possess than to be praised for the fifteen which we do possess.

The Autobiography of Mark Twain, vol. 2, p. 139. Gabriel Wells (1925).

PRAYER

Miss Watson she took me in the closet and prayed, but nothing come of it. She told me to pray every day, and whatever I asked for I would get it. But it warn't so. I tried it. Once I got a fish-line, but no hooks. It warn't any good to me without hooks.

Huck, in *Adventures of Huckleberry Finn,* ch. 3 (1885).

Pray for me! I reckon if she knowed me she'd take a job that was more nearer her size. But I bet she done it, just the same—she was just the kind. She had the grit to pray for Judus if she took the notion.

Huck, in *Adventures of Huckleberry Finn,* ch. 28 (1885).

There's something in it when a body like the widow or the parson prays, but it don't work for me, and I reckon it don't work for only just the right kind.

> Huck, in *Adventures of Huckleberry Finn*, ch. 8, pp. 52-3. Gabriel Wells (1923). First appeared in 1885.

Who prays for Satan? Who, in eighteen centuries, has had the common humanity to pray for the one sinner that needed it most?

> *The Autobiography of Mark Twain* (Neider), ch. 7, p. 28. Harper & Row (1959).

Of the 464 specifications contained in your Public Prayers for the week, and not previously noted in this report, we grant 2, and deny the rest. To wit: Granted, (1) "That the clouds may continue to perform their office; (2) and the sun his." It was the divine purpose anyhow; it will gratify you to know that you have not disturbed it.

> "Letter to the Earth," *Letters From The Earth* (1962).

If you would beseech a blessing upon yourself, beware! lest without intent you invoke a curse upon a neighbor at the same time.

> "War Prayer," *A Pen Warmed-up in Hell*, p. 90. Harper & Row (1972). Written in 1905.

PREACHERS

Aunt Sally she was one of the mixed-upest looking persons I ever see; except one, and that was uncle Silas, when he come in, and they told it all to him. It kind of made him drunk, as you may say, and he didn't know nothing at all the rest of the day, and preached a prayer meeting sermon that night that give him a rattling ruputation, because the oldest man in the world couldn't a understood it.

> Huck, in *The Adventures of Huckleberry Finn*, ch. 42 (1885).

It is not a new thing for a thoroughly good and well meaning preacher's soft heart to run away with his soft head.

> "Temperance and Woman's Rights," *Europe and Elsewhere*, p. 30. Gabriel Wells (1923).

Pride

Human pride is not worth while; there is always something lying in wait to take the wind out of it.

Following the Equator, vol. 2, "Conclusion," p. 382. Gabriel Wells (1923).

Principles

Principles is another name for prejudices.

"Literature," *Mark Twain's Speeches*, p. 207. Gabriel Wells (1923). Speech, May 4, 1900.

Principles aren't of much account anyway, except at election time. After that you hang them up to let them season.

"Municipal Corruption," *Mark Twain's Speeches*, ed. Albert Bigelow Paine (1923). Speech, January 4, 1901.

Prosperity is the best protector of principle.

"Pudd'nhead Wilson's New Calendar," *Following the Equator*, vol. 2, ch. 2, p. 13. Gabriel Wells (1923).

I find that principles have no real force except when one is well fed.

Adam, in "Wednesday," *Extracts from Adam's Diary* (1893).

Prisons

They put the beginners in with the confirmed criminals. This would be well if man were naturally inclined to good, but he isn't, and so *association* makes the beginners worse than they were when they went into captivity.

"What Is Man?" *What Is Man? and Other Philosophical Writings*, p. 164. University of California (1973).

Procrastination

Never put off till to-morrow what you can do day after to-morrow just as well.

"The Late Benjamin Franklin," *Mark Twain: Collected Tales, Sketches, Speeches, & Essays, 1852–1890*, p. 425. Library of America (1992).

*P*ROFANITY

When it comes down to pure ornamental cursing, the native American is gifted above the sons of men.

Roughing It, vol. 2, ch. 19, p. 184. Harper & Brothers (1899). Written in 1872.

*P*ROGRESS

From the beginning of the world no revolt against a public infamy or oppression has ever been begun but by the one daring man in the 10,000, the rest timidly waiting, and slowly and reluctantly joining, under the influence of that man.

"The United States of Lyncherdom," *Europe and Elsewhere*, p. 243. Gabriel Wells (1923).

*P*ROMISES

Such a very liberal amount of space was given to the organ which enables me to make promises, that the organ which should enable me to keep them was crowded out.

The Innocents Abroad, vol. 1, ch. 23, pp. 244-5. Gabriel Wells (1923). Written in 1869.

*P*ROOFREADERS

In the first place God made idiots. This was for practice. Then he made proofreaders.

Mark Twain's Notebook, p. 235. Harper & Brothers (1935). Written about 1893.

PROPHECY

A man who goes around with a prophecy-gun ought never to get discouraged. If he will keep up his heart and fire at everything he sees he is bound to hit something by and by.

The Autobiography of Mark Twain, ch. 5, p. 20. Harper & Row (1959).

Prophecies which promise valuable things, desirable things, good things, worthy things, never come true. Prophecies of this kind are like wars fought in a good cause—they are so rare that they don't count.

The Autobiography of Mark Twain, vol. 2, p. 197. Gabriel Wells (1925).

A prophet doesn't have to have any brains. They are good to have, of course, for the ordinary exigencies of life, but they are of no use in professional work. It is the restfulest vocation there is. When the spirit of prophecy comes upon you, you merely cake your intellect and lay it off in a cool place for a rest, and unship your jaw and leave it alone; it will work for itself: the result is prophecy.

A Connecticut Yankee in King Arthur's Court, ch. 27, p. 270. Gabriel Wells (1923).

He could foretell wars and famines, though that was not so hard, for there was always a war and generally a famine somewhere.

"The Mysterious Stranger," *The Portable Mark Twain*, ch. 1, p. 633. Viking (1946). Written 1897–1908.

PROSPERITY

There is an old-time toast which is golden for its beauty. "When you ascend the hill of prosperity may you not meet a friend."

"Pudd'nhead Wilson's New Calendar," *Following the Equator*, vol. 2, ch. 5, p. 48. Gabriel Wells (1923). Written in 1897.

PROVIDENCE

The proverb says that Providence protects children and idiots. This is really true. I know it because I have tested it.

The Autobiography of Mark Twain, ch. 26, p. 141. Harper & Row (1959).

There is this trouble about special providences—namely, there is so often a doubt as to which party was intended to be the beneficiary. In the case of the children, the bears, and the prophet, the bears got more real satisfaction out of the episode than the prophet did, because they got the children.

"Pudd'nhead Wilson's Calendar," *Pudd'nhead Wilson*, ch. 4, p. 26. Gabriel Wells (1923). Written in 1894.

*P*UBLIC INTEREST

No public interest is anything other or nobler than a massed accumulation of private interests.

"Dinner Speech," *Mark Twain Speaking*, p. 523. University of Iowa Press (1976). Speech, September 19, 1906.

*P*UBLIC SCHOOLS

It is curious how history repeats itself the world over. Why I remember the same thing was done when I was a boy on the Mississippi River. There was a proposition in a township there to discontinue public schools because they were too expensive. An old farmer spoke up and said if they stopped the schools they would not save anything, because every time a school was closed a jail had to be built. It's like feeding a dog on his own tail. He'll never get fat.

"Public Education Association," *Mark Twain's Speeches*, pp. 212–13. Gabriel Wells (1923). Speech, November 23, 1900.

*P*UBLIC, THE

The great public is weak-minded; the great public is sentimental; the great public always turns around and weeps for an odious murderer, and prays for him, and carries flowers to his prison, and besieges the governor with appeals to his clemency, as soon as the papers begin to howl for the man's blood.

The Gilded Age, vol. 2, ch. 12, p. 133. Harper & Brothers (1901). Written in 1873.

PUBLISHING

All publishers are Columbuses. The successful author is their America. The reflection that they—like Columbus—didn't discover what they expected to discover, didn't discover what they started out to discover, doesn't trouble them.

The Autobiography of Mark Twain (Neider), ch. 50, p. 277. Harper & Row (1959).

PUNISHMENT

Tom took his whipping and went back to his seat not at all broken-hearted, for he thought it was possible that he had unknowingly upset the ink on the spelling-book himself, in some skylarking bout—he had denied it for form's sake and because it was custom, and had stuck to the denial from principle.

The Adventures of Tom Sawyer, ch. 20 (1876).

All crimes should be punished with humiliations—public exposure in ridiculous and grotesque situations—and never in any other way. Death makes a hero of the villain.

Mark Twain's Notebook, p. 193. Harper & Brothers (1935). Written about 1888.

PUNS

The pun is like mediocre music, neither wit nor humor—and yet now and then one sees a pun which comes so near being wit that it is funny.

Mark Twain's Notebooks and Journals, vol. 2, p. 142. University of California (1975). Written July–August 1878.

QUOTATIONS

It is my belief that nearly any invented quotation, played with confidence, stands a good chance to deceive. There are some people who think that honesty is always the best policy. This is a superstition; there are times when the appearance of it is worth six of it.

Following the Equator, vol. 1, ch. 5, pp. 57-8. Gabriel Wells (1923). Written in 1897.

RADICALS

The radical invents the views. When he has worn them out the conservative adopts them.

Notebook, ch. 31, 1898 entry, ed. Albert Bigelow Paine (1935).

RANK

When we are young we generally estimate an opinion by the size of the person that holds it, but later we find that is an uncertain rule, for we realize that there are times when a hornet's opinion disturbs us more than an emperor's.

"An Undelivered Speech," *Mark Twain's Speeches*, p. 165. Gabriel Wells (1923).

READING ALOUD

The average clergyman, in all countries and of all denominations, is a very bad reader. One would think he would at least learn how to read the Lord's Prayer, by and by, but it is not so. He races through it as if he thought the quicker he got it in, the sooner it would be answered.

A Tramp Abroad, vol. 2, ch. 7, p. 93. Harper & Brothers (1899). Written in 1880.

REDHEADS

Why, man, red is the natural color of beauty! What is there that is really beautiful or grand in Nature or Art, that is not tinted with this primordial color?

"'Oh, She Has a Red Head!'" *Early Tales and Sketches*, vol. 1, p. 104. University of California (1979).

REFORM

He reckoned a body could reform the old man with a shot-gun, maybe, but he didn't know no other way.

> Huck, in *Adventures of Huckleberry Finn*, ch. 5 (1885).

It was awful thoughts, and awful words, but they was said. And I let them stay said, and never thought no more about reforming. I shoved the whole thing out of my head, and said I would take up wickedness again, which was in my line, being brung up to it, and the other warn't. And for a starter, I would go to work and steal Jim out of slavery again; and if I could think up anything worse, I would do that, too; because as long as I was in, and in for good, I might as well go the whole hog.

> Huck, in *The Adventures of Huckleberry Finn*, ch. 31 (1885).

Nothing so needs reforming as other people's habits.

> "Pudd'nhead Wilson's Calendar," *Pudd'nhead Wilson*, ch. 15 (1894).

We have pledges that make us eschew tobacco or wine, and while you are taking the pledge there is a holy influence about that makes you feel you are reformed, and that you can never be so happy again in this world until—you get outside and take a drink.

> "To the Whitefriars," *Mark Twain's Speeches*, p. 179. Gabriel Wells (1923). Speech, June 20, 1899.

REGRET

Repentance ain't confined to doing wrong, sometimes you catch it just as sharp for doing right.

> "Refuge of the Derelicts," *Mark Twain's Fables of Man*, p. 222. University of California (1972). Written between 1905 and 1906.

RELICS

As for the bones of St. Denis, I feel certain we have seen enough of them to duplicate him, if necessary.

> *The Innocents Abroad*, vol. 1, ch. 17, p. 163. Gabriel Wells (1923). Written in 1869.

RELIGION

Spiritual wants and instincts are as various in the human family as are physical appetites, complexions, and features, and a man is only at his best, morally, when he is equipped with the religious garment whose color and shape and size most nicely accommodate themselves to the spiritual complexion, angularities, and stature of the individual who wears it.

A Connecticut Yankee in King Arthur's Court, ch. 10, p. 77. Gabriel Wells (1923). Written in 1889 .

It is a good and gentle religion, but inconvenient.

Following the Equator, ch. 49 (1897).
On Hinduism.

Man is the Religious Animal. He is the only Religious Animal. He is the only animal that has the True Religion—several of them.

"Man's Place in the Animal World," *Mark Twain: Collected Tales, Sketches, Speeches, & Essays, 1891–1910*, p. 211. Library of America (1992).

I cannot see how a man of any large degree of humorous perception can ever be religious—except he purposely shut the eyes of his mind & keep them shut by force.

Mark Twain's Notebooks and Journals, vol. 3, notebook 27 (Aug. 1887–July 1888), ed. Frederick Anderson (1979).

Religion consists in a set of things which the average man thinks he believes, and wishes he was certain.

Mark Twain's Notebooks and Journals, vol. 2, p. 305. University of California (1975). Written February–September 1879.

There is no church that wouldn't break down if you took away its money power.

Mark Twain's Notebooks and Journals, vol. 3, p. 42. University of California (1979). Written Spring 1883–September 1884.

REMORSE

It was not a Southern watermelon that Eve took: we know it because she
repented.

Pudd'nhead Wilson and Those Extraordinary Twins, ch. 14 (1894).

RENAISSANCE, THE

Who is this Renaissance? Where did he come from? Who gave him
permission to cram the Republic with his execrable daubs?

The Innocents Abroad, ch. 23 (1869). On sightseeing in Venice.

REPETITION

Repetition is a mighty power in the domain of humor. If frequently used
nearly any precisely worded and unchanging formula will eventually
compel laughter if it be gravely repeated, at intervals, five or six times.

The Autobiography of Mark Twain, ch. 28, pp. 156-7. Harper & Row (1959).

REPUBLICAN PARTY, THE

Pray do not overlook our patriotism, sir. There is more of it here than
exists in any other country. It is all lodged in the Republican party. The
party will tell you so. All others are traitors, and are long ago used to
the name.

"Bishop Speech," *Mark Twain Speaking*, p. 591. University of Iowa Press (1976). Speech, October, 1907.

No one has ever seen a Republican mass meeting that was devoid of the
perception of the ludicrous.

"Turncoats," *Mark Twain's Speeches,* ed. Albert Bigelow Paine (1923). Closing words of the speech, given
in 1884.

RESOLUTIONS

I found out that a new oath holds pretty well; but that when it is become old and frayed out and damaged by a dozen annual retyings, it ceases to be serviceable; any little strain will snap it.

"On Speech-making Reform," *Mark Twain's Speeches*, p. 1. Gabriel Wells (1923). Written in 1884.

RESPECT

When people do not respect us we are sharply offended; yet deep down in his private heart no man much respects himself.

"Pudd'nhead Wilson's New Calendar," *Following the Equator*, ch. 29 (1897).

REUNIONS

It takes some time to accept and realize the fact that while you have been growing old, your friends have not been standing still, in that matter.

Life on the Mississippi , ch. 55, p. 389. Harper & Brothers (1903). Written in 1883.

REVENGE

There is an absurd idea disseminated in novels, that the happier a girl is with another man, the happier it makes the old lover she has blighted. Don't allow yourself to believe any such nonsense as that. The more cause that girl finds to regret that she did not marry you, the more comfortable you will feel over it.

"Answers to Correspondents," *Early Tales and Sketches*, vol. 2, p. 184. University of California (1981). Written in June 1865.

REVOLUTION

There were two "Reigns of Terror," if we but remember it and consider it; the one wrought murder in hot passion, the other in heartless cold blood; the one lasted mere months, the other had lasted a thousand years.

> *A Connecticut Yankee in King Arthur's Court*, ch. 13, p. 105. Gabriel Wells (1923). Written in 1889.

All gentle cant and philosophizing to the contrary notwithstanding, no people in the world ever did achieve freedom by goody-goody talk and moral suasion: it being immutable law that all revolutions that will succeed must *begin* in blood.

> *A Connecticut Yankee in King Arthur's Court*, ch. 20, p. 171. Gabriel Wells (1923). Written in 1889.

REWARDS

She was so overcome by the splendor of his achievement that she took him into the closet and selected a choice apple and delivered it to him, along with an improving lecture upon the added value and flavor a treat took to itself when it came without sin through virtuous effort. And while she closed with a Scriptural flourish, he "hooked" a doughnut.

> *The Adventures of Tom Sawyer*, ch. 3 (1876).

RIDICULE

No God and no religion can survive ridicule. No political church, no nobility, no royalty or other fraud, can face ridicule in a fair field, and live.

> *Mark Twain's Notebooks and Journals*, vol. 3, notebook 28 (July 1888–May 1889), ed. Frederick Anderson (1979).

There is no character, howsoever good and fine, but it can be destroyed by ridicule, howsoever poor and witless. Observe the ass, for instance: his character is about perfect, he is the choicest spirit among all the humbler animals, yet see what ridicule has brought him to. Instead of feeling complimented when we are called an ass, we are left in doubt.

> "Pudd'nhead Wilson's Calendar," *Pudd'nhead Wilson*, p. xix. Gabriel Wells (1923). Written in 1894.

RIGHTS

There isn't a Parallel of Latitude but thinks it would have been the Equator if it had had its rights.

Following the Equator, ch. 69 (1897).

RISK

Necessity is the mother of "taking chances."

Roughing It, vol. 2, ch. 42, p. 18. Harper & Brothers (1899). Written in 1872.

RIVERS

The face of the water, in time, became a wonderful book—a book that was a dead language to the uneducated passenger, but which told its mind to me without reserve, delivering its most cherished secrets as clearly as if it uttered them with a voice. And it was not a book to be read once and thrown aside, for it had a new story to tell every day.

Life on the Mississippi, ch. 9 (1883). Originally published as "Old Times on the Mississippi," *Atlantic Monthly* (1874). On learning to pilot a steamboat on the Mississippi.

Nonetheless, Twain went on to explain, "All the grace, the beauty, the poetry had gone out of the majestic river! . . . All the value any feature had for me now was the amount of usefulness it could furnish toward compassing the safe piloting of a steamboat."

ROME

What is there in Rome for me to see that others have not seen before me? What is there for me to touch that others have not touched? What is there for me to feel, to learn, to hear, to know, that shall thrill me before it pass to others? What can I discover?—Nothing. Nothing whatsoever. One charm of travel dies here.

The Innocents Abroad, ch. 26 (1869).

ROYALTY

All I say, is, kings is kings, and you got to make allowances. Take them all around, they're a mighty ornery lot. It's the way they're raised.

> Huck, in *The Adventures of Huckleberry Finn*, ch. 23 (1885).

No throne exists that has a right to exist, and no symbol of it, flying from any flagstaff, is righteously entitled to wear any device but the skull and crossbones of that kindred industry which differs from royalty only businesswise—merely as retail differs from wholesale.

> *The American Claimant*, ch. 10 (1892).

It is enough to make a body ashamed of his race to think of the sort of froth that has always occupied its thrones without a shadow of right or reason, and the seventh-rate people that have always figured as its aristocracies—a company of monarchs and nobles who, as a rule, would have achieved only poverty and obscurity if left, like their betters, to their own designs.

> *A Connecticut Yankee in King Arthur's Court*, ch. 2, p. 16. Gabriel Wells (1923). Written in 1889 .

A monarch, when good, is entitled to the consideration which we accord to a pirate who keeps Sunday School between crimes; when bad, he is entitled to none at all.

> *Mark Twain's Notebooks and Journals*, vol. 3, notebook 28 (July 1888–May 1889), ed. Frederick Anderson (1979).

SATAN

I have no special regard for Satan; but I can at least claim that I have no prejudice against him. It may even be that I lean a little his way, on account of his not having a fair show. All religions issue bibles against him, and say the most injurious things about him, but we never hear *his* side.

> "Concerning the Jews," *Harper's* (New York, Sept. 1899), repr. in *Complete Essays,* ed. Charles Neider (1963).

We may not pay Satan reverence, for that would be indiscreet, but we can at least respect his talents. A person who has for untold centuries maintained the imposing position of spiritual head of four-fifths of the human race, and political head of the whole of it, must be granted the possession of executive abilities of the loftiest order.

"Concerning the Jews," *Harper's* (New York, Sept. 1899), repr. in *Complete Essays,* ed. Charles Neider (1963).

SATIETY

It is a pleasure to watch a company of gentlemen in that condition which is peculiar to gentlemen who have had their dinners. That was a time when the real nature of man came out.

"Dinner Speech," *Mark Twain Speaking,* p. 429. University of Iowa Press (1976). Speech, March 8, 1902.

SATIRE

Out of the unconscious lips of babes and sucklings are we satirized.

"Which Was the Dream?" (written 1897), published in *Which Was the Dream?* ed. John S. Tuckey (1967).

SCHOOL BOARDS

In the first place God made idiots. This was for practice. Then He made School Boards.

"Pudd'nhead Wilson's New Calendar," *Following the Equator,* ch. 61 (1897).

SCIENCE

Scientists have odious manners, except when you prop up their theory; then you can borrow money of them.

The Bee (1917), repr. in *Complete Essays,* ed. Charles Neider (1963).

There is something fascinating about science. One gets such wholesale returns of conjecture out of such a trifling investment of fact.

> *Life on the Mississippi*, ch. 17 (1883). Originally published as "Old Times on the Mississippi," *Atlantic Monthly* (1874).

SCRIPTURE

The Christian's Bible is a drug store. Its contents remain the same; but the medical practice changes.

> "Bible Teaching and Religious Practice," *A Pen Warmed-up in Hell*, p. 138. Harper & Row (1972). Written in 1890.

SEAFARING

Ours was a reasonably comfortable ship, with the customary seagoing fare—plenty of good food furnished by the Deity and cooked by the Devil.

> *Following the Equator*, vol. 1, ch. 1, p. 2. Gabriel Wells (1923). Written in 1897.

SEASICKNESS

If there is one thing in the world that will make a man peculiarly and insufferably self-conceited, it is to have his stomach behave itself, the first day at sea, when nearly all his comrades are seasick.

> *The Innocents Abroad*, vol. 1, ch. 3, p. 17. Gabriel Wells (1923). Written in 1869.

SEASONS

Change is the handmaiden Nature requires to do her miracles with. The land with four well-defined seasons cannot lack beauty, or pall with monotony.

> *Roughing It*, vol. 2, ch. 15, p. 150. Harper & Brothers (1899). Written in 1872.

SELF-CONTROL

When angry, count four; when very angry, swear.

"Pudd'nhead Wilson's Calendar," *Pudd'nhead Wilson,* ch. 10 (1894).

SELF-DECEPTION

We do not deal much in facts when we are contemplating ourselves.

"Does the Race of Man Love a Lord?" *Mark Twain: Collected Tales, Sketches, Speeches & Essays: 1891–1910,* p. 522. Library of America (1992). Written in April, 1902.

SELF-DISCIPLINE

Franklin said once, in one of his inspired flights of malignity: "Early to bed and early to rise/Makes a man healthy and wealthy and wise." As if it were any object to a boy to be healthy and wealthy and wise on such terms.

"The Late Benjamin Franklin," *Sketches Old and New*, pp. 212–3. Harper & Brothers (1903). Written in July 1870.

SELF-ESTEEM

If everybody was satisfied with himself there would be no heroes.

The Autobiography of Mark Twain, vol. 1, p. 264. Gabriel Wells (1925).

SELF-HATRED

We can secure other people' approval, if we do right and try hard; but our own is worth a hundred of it, and no way has been found out of securing that.

"Pudd'nhead Wilson's New Calendar," *Following the Equator*, vol. 1, ch. 14, p. 131. Gabriel Wells (1923). Written in 1897.

SENSITIVITY

We think boys are rude, unsensitive animals but it is not so in all cases. Each boy has one or two sensitive spots and if you can find out where they are located you have only to touch them and you can scorch him as with fire.

The Autobiography of Mark Twain, vol. 1, p. 128. Gabriel Wells (1925).

SENTIMENTALITY

As the two boys walked sorrowing along, they made a new compact to stand by each other and be brothers and never separate till death relieved them of their troubles. Then they began to lay their plans. Joe was for being a hermit, and living on crusts in a remote cave, and dying, some time, of cold, and want, and grief; but after listening to Tom, he conceded that there were some conspicuous advantages about a life of crime, and so he consented to be a pirate.

The Adventures of Tom Sawyer, ch. 13 (1876).

SERMONS

It was an argument that dealt in limitless fire and brimstone and thinned the predestined elect down to a company so small as to be hardly worth saving.

The Adventures of Tom Sawyer, ch. 5, p. 62. Harper & Brothers (1903). Written in 1876.

SEX

[Man] has imagined a heaven, and has left entirely out of it the supremest of all his delights, the one ecstasy that stands first and foremost in the heart of every individual of his race—and ours—sexual intercourse! It is as if a lost and perishing person in a roasting desert should be told by a rescuer he might choose and have all longed for things but one, and he should elect to leave out water!

> Satan, in *Letters from the Earth*, p. 8 (1962).

The law of God, as quite plainly expressed in woman's construction, is this: There shall be no limit put upon your intercourse with the other sex sexually, at any time of life. . . . During twenty-three days in every month (in the absence of pregnancy) from the time a woman is seven years old till she dies of old age, she is ready for action, and *competent*. As competent as the candlestick is to receive the candle. Competent every day, competent every night. Also, she *wants* that candle—yearns for it, longs for it, hankers after it, as commanded by the law of God in her heart.

> Satan, in *Letters from the Hearth*, letter 8, ed. Bernard De Voto (1962).
>
> As for men, "The law of god, as quite plainly expressed in man's construction, is this: During your entire life you shall be under inflexible limits and restrictions, sexually."

SHAKESPEARE

To be or not to be; that is the bare bodkin.

> *Adventures of Huckleberry Finn*, ch. 21, p. 190. Gabriel Wells (1923). The Duke of Bilgewater interpreting *Hamlet*. First appeared in 1885.

SISTERS

You ought never to knock your little sisters down with a club. It is better to use a cat, which is soft. In doing this you must be careful to take the cat by the tail in such a manner that she cannot scratch you.

> "Advice for Good Little Boys," *Early Tales and Sketches*, vol. 2, p. 242. University of California (1981). Written in 1865.

SKILL

There is some dignity about an acquirement, because it is a product of your own labor. It is wages earned, whereas to be able to do a thing merely by the grace of God and not by your own effort transfers the distinction to our heavenly home—where possibly it is a matter of pride and satisfaction but it leaves you naked and bankrupt.

> *The Autobiography of Mark Twain*, vol. 2, p. 257. Gabriel Wells (1925).

SLANDER

A feeble, stupid, preposterous lie will not live two years—except it be a slander upon somebody.

"Advice to Youth," *Mark Twain Speaking*, p.170. University of Iowa Press (1976). Speech, April 15, 1882.

Few slanders can stand the wear of silence.

> *The Autobiography of Mark Twain*, vol. 1, p. 139. Gabriel Wells (1925).

SLEEP

Go to bed early, get up early—this is wise. Some authorities say get up with the sun; some others say get up with one thing, some with another. But a lark is really the best thing to get up with. It gives you a splendid reputation with everybody to know that you get up with the lark; and if you get the right kind of lark, and work at him right, you can easily train him to get up at half past nine.

> "Advice to Youth," *Mark Twain's Speeches*, p. 105. Gabriel Wells (1923). Written about 1882.

"It is the early bird that catches the worm." It is a seductive proposition, and well calculated to trap the unsuspecting. But its attractions are all wasted on me, because I have no use for the worm.

> "Early Rising, As Regards Excursions to the Cliff House," *Early Tales and Sketches*, vol. 2, p. 25. University of California (1981). Written in July 1864.

SMOKING

As an example to others, and not that I care for moderation, it has always been my rule never to smoke when asleep, and never to refrain when awake.

"Seventieth Birthday," *Mark Twain's Speeches*, p. 258. Gabriel Wells (1923). Speech, December 5, 1905.

SOCIAL STATUS

We adore titles and heredities in our hearts and ridicule them with our mouths. This is our democratic privilege.

The Autobiography of Mark Twain, vol. 2, p. 350. Gabriel Wells (1925).

SOUL, THE

Be careless in your dress if you must, but keep a tidy soul.

Following the Equator, ch. 23 (1897).

A great soul, with a great purpose, can make a weak body strong and keep it so.

Joan of Arc, bk. 2, ch. 4, p. 87. Harper & Brothers. Written in 1896.

SPEECHMAKING

The really important matter, perhaps, is that the speaker make himself reasonably interesting while he is on his feet, and avoid exasperating the people who are not privileged to make speeches, and also not privileged to get out of the way when the other people begin.

The Autobiography of Mark Twain, vol. 1, pp. 278–79. Gabriel Wells (1925).

Written things are not for speech; their form is literary; they are stiff, inflexible and will not lend themselves to happy and effective delivery with the tongue—where their purpose is to merely entertain, not instruct; they have to be limbered up, broken up, colloquialized and turned into the common forms of unpremeditated talk.

   The Autobiography of Mark Twain, ch. 35, p. 192. Harper & Row (1959).

I am not one of those geniuses who can make a speech *impromptu*. I have made a great many happy impromptu speeches but I had time to prepare them.

   "Dinner Speech," *Mark Twain Speaking*, p. 65. University of Iowa Press (1976). Speech, February 1872.

The best and most telling speech is not the actual impromptu one, but the counterfeit of it.

   "On Speechmaking Reform," *Mark Twain Speaking*, p. 191. University of Iowa Press (1976). Speech, March 31, 1885.

There's a great deal moral difference between a lecture and a speech, I can tell you. For when you deliver a lecture you get good pay, but when you make a speech you don't get a cent.

   "Political Speech," *Mark Twain Speaking*, p. 139. University of Iowa Press (1976). Speech, October 26, 1880.

You ought never to have any part of the audience behind you; you can never tell what they are going to do.

   "Remarks," *Mark Twain Speaking*, p. 619. University of Iowa Press (1976). Speech, April 18, 1908.

SPELLING

I never had any large respect for good spelling. That is my feeling yet. Before the spelling book came with its arbitrary forms, men unconsciously revealed shades of their characters and also added enlightening shades of expression to what they wrote by their spelling, and so it is possible that the spelling book has been a doubtful benevolence to us.

   The Autobiography of Mark Twain, vol. 2, p. 68. Gabriel Wells (1925).

Some people have an idea that correct spelling can be *taught*—and taught to anybody. That is a mistake. The spelling faculty is born in a man, like poetry, music, and art. It is a gift; it is a talent.

"Introductory Remarks," *Mark Twain Speaking*, p. 95. University of Iowa Press (1976). Speech, May 12, 1875.

S*PITE*

There is more real pleasure to be gotten out of a malicious act, where your heart is in it, than out of thirty acts of a nobler sort.

The Autobiography of Mark Twain, ch. 77, p. 395. Harper & Row (1959).

S*T. LOUIS*

"If you send a d__d fool to St. Louis, and you don't tell them he's a d__d fool, *they'll* never find it out. There's one thing sure—if I had a d__d fool I should know what to do with him. Ship him to St. Louis—it's the noblest market in the world for that kind of property."

Life on the Mississippi, ch. 53 (1883). Originally published as "Old Times on the Mississippi," *Atlantic Monthly* (1874).

Attributed by Twain to a resident of Hannibal, Missouri. First appeared in 1883.

S*TATISTICS*

Sometimes half a dozen figures will reveal, as with a lightning-flash, the importance of a subject which ten thousand labored words, with the same purpose in view, had left at last but dim and uncertain.

Life on the Mississippi, ch. 53 (1883). Originally published as "Old Times on the Mississippi," *Atlantic Monthly* (1874).

S*TUPIDITY*

His head was an hour-glass; it could stow an idea, but it had to do it a grain at a time, not the whole idea at once.

A Connecticut Yankee in King Arthur's Court, ch. 28, p. 277. Gabriel Wells (1923). Written in 1889 .

S*UBMISSIVENESS*

To create man was a fine and original idea; but to add the sheep was a tautology.

Mark Twain's Notebook, p. 379. Harper & Brothers (1935). Written about 1902.

S*UCCESS*

It is strange the way the ignorant and inexperienced so often and undeservedly succeed when the informed and the experienced fail.

The Autobiography of Mark Twain (Neider), ch. 45, p. 254. Harper & Row (1959).

S*UPERIORITY*

There it is: it doesn't make any difference who we are or what we are, there's always *somebody* to look down on! somebody to hold in light esteem, somebody to be indifferent about.

"Three Thousand Years Among the Microbes," *Which Was the Dream?,* ch. 15, ed. John S. Tuckey (written 1905, publ. 1967).

S*UPERSTITION*

I've always reckoned that looking at the new moon over your left shoulder is one of the carelessest and foolishest things a body can do. Old Hank Bunker done it once, and bragged about it; and in less than two years he got drunk and fell off of the shot tower and spread himself out so that he was just a kind of layer, as you may say; and they slid him edgeways between two barn doors for a coffin, and buried him so, so they say, but I didn't see it. Pap told me. But anyway, it all come of looking at the moon that way, like a fool.

> Huck, in *Adventures of Huckleberry Finn*, ch. 10 (1885).

Jim said bees wouldn't sting idiots; but I didn't believe that, because I had tried them lots of times myself, and they wouldn't sting me.

> Huck, in *Adventures of Huckleberry Finn*, ch. 8 (1885).

When the human race has once acquired a superstition nothing short of death is ever likely to remove it.

> *The Autobiography of Mark Twain*, ch. 78, p. 402. Harper & Row (1959).

Let me make the superstitions of a nation and I care not who makes its laws or its songs either.

> *Following the Equator*, ch. 51 (1897).

*S*WEARING

In certain trying circumstances, urgent circumstances, desperate circumstances, profanity furnishes a relief denied even to prayer.

> *Mark Twain: A Biography* (Paine), vol. 1, p. 214. Gabriel Wells (1923).

*T*ALENT

The lowest intellect, like the highest, possesses a skill of some kind and takes a keen pleasure in testing it, proving it, perfecting it.

> *Letters from the Earth*, Letter 2, p. 9. Harper & Row (1962). Written in 1909.

If you have no natural gift for art, then it is not worth while to meddle with art. If you have a natural gift, it is not going to be valuable until you have the right teaching.

> "Speech on Art," *Mark Twain Speaking*, p. 444. University of Iowa Press (1976). Speech, June 7, 1902.

TALK

Noise proves nothing. Often a hen who has laid an egg cackles as if she had laid an asteroid.

"Pudd'nhead Wilson's New Calendar," *Following the Equator*, vol. 1, ch. 5, p. 56. Gabriel Wells (1923). Written in 1897.

TAXES

What is the difference between a taxidermist and a tax collector? The taxidermist takes only your skin.

Mark Twain's Notebook, p. 379. Harper & Brothers (1935). Written about 1902.

I know all those people. I have friendly, social, and criminal relations with the whole lot of them.

"Taxes and Morals," published in *Complete Essays of Mark Twain,* ed. Charles Neider (1963). Speech, Jan. 22, 1906, Carnegie Hall, New York City. Concerning tax evaders.

We've got so much taxation. I don't know of a single foreign product that enters this country untaxed except the answer to prayer.

"When in Doubt, Tell the Truth," *Mark Twain's Speeches*, p. 293. Gabriel Wells (1923). Speech, March 9, 1906.

TEMPER

It takes me a long time to lose my temper, but once lost I could not find it with a dog.

Mark Twain's Notebook, p. 240. Harper & Brothers (1935). Written about 1894.

TEMPTATION

Down a piece, abreast the house, stood a little log cabin against the rail fence; and there the woody hill fell sharply away . . . to a limpid brook . . . a divine place for wading, and it had swimming pools too, which were

forbidden to us and therefore much frequented by us. For we were little
Christian children and had early been taught the value of forbidden fruit.

> *The Autobiography of Mark Twain*, vol. 1, p. 99. Gabriel Wells (1925).

There are several good protections against temptations but the surest is
cowardice.

> "Pudd'nhead Wilson's New Calendar," *Following the Equator*, ch. 36 (1897). The epigram also appears as
> an entry, 1898, in Twain *Notebook*, ch. 31, ed. Albert Bigelow Paine (1935).

It was not that Adam ate the apple for the apple's sake, but because it was
forbidden. It would have been better for us—oh infinitely better for us—if
the *serpent* had been forbidden .

> *Mark Twain's Notebook*, p. 275. Harper & Brothers (1935). Written about 1896.

*T*HEFT

Pap always said it warn't no harm to borrow things, if you was meaning to
pay them back, sometime; but the widow said it warn't anything but a soft
name for stealing, and no decent body would do it. Jim said he reckoned
the widow was partly right and pap was partly right; so the best way would
be for us to pick out two or three things from the list and say we wouldn't
borrow them any more—then he reckoned it wouldn't be no harm to
borrow the others. So we talked it over all one night, drifting on down the
river, trying to make up our minds whether to drop the watermelons, or
the cantelopes, or the mushmelons, or what. But toward daylight, we got it
all settled satisfactory, and concluded to drop crabapples and p'simmons.

> Huck, in *Adventures of Huckleberry Finn*, ch. 12 (1885).

Sometimes I lifted a chicken that warn't roosting comfortable, and took
him along. Pap always said, take a chicken when you get a chance, because
if you don't want him yourself you can easy find somebody that does, and
a good deed ain't ever forgot. I never see pap when he didn't want the
chicken himself, but that is what he used to say, anyway.

> Huck, in *Adventures of Huckleberry Finn*, ch. 12 (1885).

You ought never to take anything that don't belong to you—if you can not
carry it off.

> "Advice for Good Little Boys," *Early Tales and Sketches*, vol. 2, p. 242. University of California (1981).
> Written in 1865.

I know the taste of the watermelon which has been honestly come by, and I know the taste of the watermelon that has been acquired by art. Both taste good, but the experienced know which tastes best.

> *The Autobiography of Mark Twain*, vol. 1, p. 111. Gabriel Wells (1925).

THEOLOGY

There was never a century nor a country that was short of experts who knew the Deity's mind and were willing to reveal it.

> "As Concerns Interpreting the Deity," repr. in *What Is Man?*, ed. Paul Baender (1973). Written in 1905.

We have infinite trouble in solving man-made mysteries; it is only when we set out to discover the secret of God that our difficulties disappear.

> "As Concerns Interpreting the Deity," *What Is Man? and Other Philosophical Essays*, p. 111. University of California (1973). Written in 1905.

THRIFT

Simple rules for saving money: To save half, when you are fired by an eager impulse to contribute to a charity, wait, and count forty. To save three-quarters, count sixty. To save it all, count sixty-five.

> "Pudd'nhead Wilson's New Calendar," *Following the Equator*, vol. 2, ch. 11, p. 112. Gabriel Wells (1923). Written in 1897.

TIME

Geological time is not money.

> "More Maxims of Mark," *Mark Twain: Collected Tales, Sketches, Speeches, & Essays, 1891–1910*, p. 942. Library of America (1992).

TITLES

My book is not named yet. Have to write it first—you wouldn't make a garment for an animal till you had seen the animal, would you?

Mark Twain's Letters, vol. 4 p. 208. University of California (1995). Letter, dated October 13, 1870, to Mary Fairbanks, a close friend, referring to *Roughing It*.

TOLERANCE

Reverence for one's own sacred things—parents, religion, flag, laws, and respect for one's own beliefs—these are feelings which we cannot even help. They come natural to us; they are involuntary, like breathing. There is no personal merit in breathing. But the reverence which is difficult, and which has personal merit in it, is the respect which you pay, without compulsion to the political or religious attitude of a man whose beliefs are not yours.

Following the Equator, vol. 2, ch. 17, pp. 192–3. Gabriel Wells (1923). Written in 1897.

TOURISTS AND TOURIST ATTRACTIONS

When a thing is a wonder to us it is not because of what *we* see in it, but because of what *others* have seen in it. We get almost all of our wonders at second hand.

Following the Equator, vol. 2, ch. 17, p. 185. Gabriel Wells (1923). Written in 1897.

You perceive I generalize with intrepidity from single instances. It is the tourist's custom.

Mark Twain's Notebooks and Journals, vol. 2, notebook 18, ed. Frederick Anderson (1975).

TRAGEDY

To leave that powerful agency out is to haul the culture-wagon with a crippled team.

"About Play-Acting," *The Man that Corrupted Hadleyburg and Other Stories and Essays*, p. 249. Harper & Brothers (1900). Bemoaning the underdevelopment of tragic drama in the U.S. First published in October 1898.

TRAINING

Arguments have no chance against petrified training; they wear it as little as the waves wear a cliff.

A Connecticut Yankee in King Arthur's Court, ch. 18, p. 150. Gabriel Wells (1923).

In morals, conduct, and beliefs we take the color of our environment and associations, and it is a color that can be safely warranted to wash.

"Is Shakespeare Dead?" *What Is Man and Other Essays*, p. 365. Harper & Brothers, 1917. Written in 1909.

Training is everything. The peach was once a bitter almond; cauliflower is nothing but cabbage with a college education.

"Pudd'nhead Wilson's Calendar," *Pudd'nhead Wilson*, ch. 5 (1894).

TRANSLATION

Translations always reverse a thing and bring an entirely new side of it into view, thus doubling the property and making two things out of what was only one.

"On After-dinner Speaking," *Mark Twain's Speeches*, p. 83. Gabriel Wells (1923). Written in 1880.

I have a prejudice against people who print things in a foreign language and add no translation. When I am the reader, and the other considers me able to do the translating myself, he pays me quite a nice compliment—but if he would do the translating for me I would try to get along without the compliment.

A Tramp Abroad, vol. 1, ch. 16, p. 140. Harper & Brothers (1899). Written in 1880.

TRAVELING AND TRAVELERS

To forget pain is to be painless; to forget care is to be rid of it; to go abroad is to accomplish both.

The Autobiography of Mark Twain, vol. 2, pp. 234-5. Gabriel Wells (1925).

For a tranquil pleasure excursion, there was nothing equal to a raft.

"Facts Concerning the Recent Resignation," *Sketches Old and New*, p. 349. Harper & Brothers (1903).

The nomadic instinct is a human instinct; it was born with Adam and transmitted to the patriarchs, and after thirty centuries of steady effort, civilization has not educated it entirely out of us yet.

The Innocents Abroad, vol. 2, ch. 28, p. 334. Gabriel Wells (1923). Written in 1869.

There is nothing here [Civita Vecchia] to see. They have not even a cathedral, with eleven tons of solid silver archbishops in the back room; and they do not show you any moldy buildings that are seven thousand years old; nor any smoke-dried old fire-screens which are *chef d'oeuvres* of Rubens or Simpson, or Titian or Ferguson, or any of those parties; and they haven't any bottled fragments of saints, and not even a nail from the true cross. We are going to Rome. There is nothing to see here.

Innocents Abroad, ch. 25, American Publishing Company (1869).

Too often we have been glad when it was time to go home and be distressed no more about illustrious localities.

The Innocents Abroad, vol. 2, ch. 27, p. 327. Gabriel Wells (1923).

Travel and experience mar the grandest pictures and rob us of the most cherished traditions.

The Innocents Abroad, vol. 2, ch. 28, p. 345. Gabriel Wells (1923). Written in 1869.

We wish to learn all the curious, outlandish ways of all the different countries, so that we can "show off" and astonish people when we get home. We wish to excite the envy of our untraveled friends with our strange foreign fashions which we can't shake off. All our passengers are paying strict attention to this thing, with the end in view which I have mentioned. The gentle reader will never, never know what a consummate ass he can become, until he goes abroad.

Innocents Abroad, ch. 23, American Publishing Company (1869).

If you are of any account, stay at home and make your way by faithful diligence; but if you are "no account," go away from home, and then you will *have* to work, whether you want to or not. Thus you become a blessing to your friends by ceasing to be a nuisance to them—if the people you go among suffer by the operation.

Roughing It, vol. 2, ch. 38, p. 339. Harper & Brothers (1899). Written in 1872.

It was a comfort in those succeeding days to sit up and contemplate the majestic panorama of mountains and valleys spread out below us and eat ham and hard boiled eggs while our spiritual natures reveled alternately in rainbows, thunderstorms, and peerless sunsets. Nothing helps scenery like ham and eggs.

Roughing It, p 139, American Publishing Company (1871).

I have found out that there ain't no surer way to find out whether you like people or hate them than to travel with them.

Tom Sawyer Abroad, ch. 11 (1894).

A man accustomed to American food and American cookery would not starve to death suddenly in Europe; but I think he would gradually waste away, and eventually die.

A Tramp Abroad , vol. 2., ch. 20, p. 258. Harper & Brothers (1899). Written in 1880.

T*RUTH*

I reckon a body that ups and tells the truth when he is in a tight place, is taking considerable many resks; though I ain't had no experience, and can't say for certain.

Huck, in *The Adventures of Huckleberry Finn*, ch. 28 (1885).

Truth is mighty and will prevail. There is nothing the matter with this, except that it ain't so.

Mark Twain's Notebook, p. 345. Harper & Brothers (1935). Written about 1898.

Proof once established is better left so.

"The Man that Corrupted Hadleyburg," *The Man that Corrupted Hadleyburg and Other Stories and Essays*, p. 30. Harper & Brothers (1900).

Familiarity breeds contempt. How accurate that is. The reason we hold truth in such respect is because we have so little opportunity to get familiar with it.

> *Notebook*, ch. 31, entry for 1898, ed. Albert Bigelow Paine (1935).

An injurious lie is an uncommendable thing; and so, also, and in the same degree, is an injurious truth.

> "On the Decay of the Art of Lying," (1882).

Truth is the most valuable thing we have. Let us economize it.

> "Pudd'nhead Wilson's New Calendar," ch. 7, *Following the Equator* (1897).

The report of my death was an exaggeration.

> *Mark Twain's Notebook* (1935).

> This line has been quoted in various ways, more powerfully, I think, as "The report of my death has been greatly exaggerated." Since it was quoted by the newspapers, it is difficult to know what Twain's exact phrasing was when he invented the line. Originally a response to a newspaper reporter's inquiry about a rumor that Twain was either dead or on his deathbed in London, 1896.

*T*RUTH-SEEKERS

There have been innumerable Temporary Seekers after the Truth—have you ever heard of a permanent one?

> "What Is Man?" *What Is Man? and Other Philosophical Writings*, p. 162. University of California (1973). Written in 1906.

*T*WAIN, MARK

There are artists and artists—I am one of the latter kind.

> *Mark Twain's Notebooks and Journals*, vol. 2, p. 250. University of California (1975). Written October 1878–February 1879.

*U*NPOPULARITY

I couldn't have raised an audience with a sheriff.

> *A Connecticut Yankee in King Arthur's Court*, ch. 7, p. 59. Gabriel Wells (1923). Written in 1889.

Venice

This the famed gondola and this the gorgeous gondolier!—the one an inky, rusty old canoe with a sable hearse-body clapped on to the middle of it, and the other a mangy, barefooted gutter-snipe with a portion of his raiment on exhibition which should have been sacred from public scrutiny.

The Innocents Abroad, vol. 1, ch. 22, p. 219. Gabriel Wells (1923). Written in 1869.

Virtue

Virtue never has been as respectable as money.

The Innocents Abroad, vol. 2, ch. 28, p. 336. Gabriel Wells (1923). Written in 1869.

Vocations

It is human nature to yearn to be what we were never intended for.

Mark Twain's Letters, vol. 1 p. 323. University of California (1988). Letter, dated October 19, 1865, to Orion and Mollie Clemens, Twain's brother and sister-in-law.

Vulgarity

There are no people who are quite so vulgar as the over-refined ones.

"Pudd'nhead Wilson's New Calendar," *Following the Equator*, vol. 2, ch. 26, p. 285. Gabriel Wells (1923). Written in 1897.

War

A wanton waste of projectiles.

"The Benefit of Judicious Training," *Mark Twain Speaking*, p. 153. University of Iowa Press (1976). Referring to war, June 8, 1881.

It seemed an epitome of war; that all war must be just that—the killing of strangers against whom you feel no personal animosity.

"The Private History of a Campaign that Failed," *A Pen Warmed-up in Hell*, p. 23. Harper & Row (1972). Written in December 1885.

WARFARE

When I retired from the rebel army in '61 I retired upon Louisiana in good order; at least in good enough order for a person who had not yet learned how to retreat according to the rules of war, and had to trust to native genius. It seemed to me that for a first attempt at a retreat it was not badly done. I had done no advancing in that campaign that was at all equal to it.

Life on the Mississippi, ch. 53 (1883). Originally published as "Old Times on the Mississippi," *Atlantic Monthly* (1874).

WASHINGTON, GEORGE

The idea that his father was overjoyed when he told little George that he would rather have him cut down a thousand cherry trees than tell a lie is all nonsense. What did he really mean? Why, that he was absolutely astonished that he had a son who had the chance to tell a lie and didn't.

"Dinner Speech," *Mark Twain Speaking*, p. 484. University of Iowa Press (1976). Speech, February 7, 1902.

WASHINGTON, D.C.

There is something good and motherly about Washington, the grand old benevolent National Asylum for the Helpless.

The Gilded Age, vol. 1, ch. 24, p. 269. Harper & Brothers (1901). Written in 1873.

WASTE

Spending one's capital is feeding a dog on his own tail.

> *Mark Twain's Notebook*, p. 345. Harper & Brothers (1935). Written about 1898.

WATCHES

When your watch gets out of order you have choice of two things to do: throw it in the fire or take it to the watch-tinker. The former is the quickest.

> "Pudd'nhead Wilson's New Calendar," *Following the Equator*, vol. 2, ch. 28, p. 306. Gabriel Wells (1923). Written in 1897.

WATERMELONS

The true Southern watermelon is a boon apart, and not to be mentioned with commoner things. It is chief of this world's luxuries, king by the grace of God over all the fruits of the earth. When one has tasted it, he knows what the angels eat. It was not a Southern watermelon that Eve took; we know it because she repented.

> "Pudd'nhead Wilson's Calendar," *Pudd'nhead Wilson*, ch. 14, p. 117. Gabriel Wells (1923). Written in 1894.

WEALTH

I think the reason why we Americans seem to be so addicted to trying to get rich suddenly is merely because the *opportunity* to make promising efforts in that direction has offered itself to us with a frequency out of all proportion to the European experience.

> "What Paul Bourget Thinks of Us," *How to Tell a Story and Other Essays*, p. 199. Harper & Brothers, 1897. Written in 1895.

WINTER

It is a time when one's spirit is subdued and sad, one knows not why; when the past seems a storm-swept desolation, life a vanity and a burden, and the future but a way to death.

The Gilded Age, vol. 2, ch. 60, p. 317. Harper & Brothers (1901). Referrring to winter. First appeared in 1873.

WISDOM

Education consists mainly in what we have unlearned.

Mark Twain's Notebook, p. 346 . Harper & Brothers (1935). Written about 1898.

WOMEN

Nothing is so ignorant as a man's left hand, except a lady's watch.

"Pudd'nhead Wilson's New Calendar," *Following the Equator*, vol. 1, ch. 22, p. 193. Gabriel Wells (1923). Written in 1897.

She is precious; as a wet-nurse, she has no equal among men.

"Woman—An Opinion," *Mark Twain's Speeches*, p. 32. Gabriel Wells (1923).

WOMEN'S LIBERATION

I feel persuaded that in extending the suffrage to women this country could lose absolutely nothing and might gain a great deal. For thirty centuries history has been iterating and reiterating that in a moral fight woman is simply dauntless, and we all know, even with our eyes shut upon Congress and our voters, that from the day Adam ate of the apple and told on Eve down to the present day, man, in a moral fight, has pretty uniformly shown himself to be an arrant coward.

"Temperance and Woman's Rights," *Europe and Elsewhere*, p. 30. Gabriel Wells (1923). Written in 1873.

WORK

My idea is that the employer should be the busy man, and the employee the idle one. The employer should be the worried man, and the employee the happy one. And why not? He gets the salary.

"Business," *Mark Twain's Speeches*, p. 236. Gabriel Wells (1923). Speech, March 30, 1901.

There are wise people who talk ever so knowingly and complacently about "the working classes," and satisfy themselves that a day's hard intellectual work is very much harder than a day's hard manual toil, and is righteously entitled to a much bigger pay. Why, they really think that, you know, because they know all about the one, but haven't tried the other. But I know all about both; so far as I am concerned, there isn't enough money in the universe to hire me to swing a pickax thirty days, but I will do the hardest kind of intellectual work for just as near as nothing as you can cipher it down.

A Connecticut Yankee in King Arthur's Court, ch. 22, p. 200. Gabriel Wells (1923). Written in 1889.

We know all about the habits of the ant, we know all about the habits of the bee, but we know nothing at all about the habits of the oyster. It seems almost certain that we have been choosing the wrong time for studying the oyster.

"Pudd'nhead Wilson's Calendar," *Pudd'nhead Wilson*, ch. 16, p. 142. Gabriel Wells (1923). Written in 1894.

WRITERS

A man is always better than his presented opinions. A man always reserves to himself on the inside a purity and an honesty and a justice that are a credit to him, whereas the things he prints are just the reverse.

"Dinner to Hamilton W. Mabie," *Mark Twain's Speeches*, p. 240. Gabriel Wells (1923). Speech, April 29, 1901.

WRITING

If I'd 'a' knowed what a trouble it was to make a book I wouldn't 'a' tackled it, and ain't a-going to no more.

> Huck, in *Adventures of Huckleberry Finn*, "Chapter the Last," p. 405. Gabriel Wells (1923). First appeared in 1885.

I have always been able to gain my living without doing any work; for the writing of books and magazine matter was always play, not work. I enjoyed it; it was merely billiards to me.

> *The Autobiography of Mark Twain*, ch. 60, p. 318. Harper & Row (1959).

My uncle, John A. Quarles, was also a farmer. . . . I have never consciously used him or his wife in a book but his farm has come very handy to me in literature once or twice. In *Huck Finn* and in *Tom Sawyer, Detective* I moved it down to Arkansas. It was all of six hundred miles but it was no trouble; it was not a very large farm. . . . And as for the morality of it, I cared nothing for that; I would move a state if the exigencies of literature required it.

> *The Autobiography of Mark Twain*, vol. 1, p. 96. Gabriel Wells (1925).

There are some books that refuse to be written. They stand their ground year after year and will not be persuaded. It isn't because the book is not there and worth being written—it is only because the right form for the story does not present itself. There is only one right form for a story and if you fail to find that form the story will not tell itself.

> The *Autobiography of Mark Twain*, pp. 266–67. Harper & Brothers, 1917.

It is a good thing, perhaps, to write for the amusement of the public, but it is a far higher and nobler thing to write for their instruction.

> "Curing a Cold," *Sketches Old and New*, p. 396. Harper & Brothers (1903). Written on September 20, 1863.

To my mind that literature is best and most enduring which is characterized by a noble simplicity.

> "Dinner Speech," *Mark Twain Speaking*, p. 160. University of Iowa Press (1976). Speech, December 8, 1881.

Experience is an author's most valuable asset; experience is the thing that puts the muscle and the breath and the warm blood into the book he writes.

"Is Shakespeare Dead?" *What Is Man and Other Essays*, p. 318. Harper & Brothers, 1917. Written in 1909.

It takes a heap of sense to write good nonsense.

Mark Twain's Notebooks and Journals, vol. 2, p. 303. University of California (1975). Written February–September 1879.

YOUTH

Consider well the proportions of things. It is better to be a young June-bug than an old bird of paradise.

"Pudd'nhead Wilson's Calendar," *Pudd'nhead Wilson*, ch. 8, p. 56. Gabriel Wells (1923). Written in 1894.

Whatever a man's age, he can reduce it several years by putting a bright-colored flower in his button-hole.

The American Claimant, ch. 20, p. 177. Harper & Brothers, 1896. Written in 1892.